Privatisation in India

This book is a comprehensive work which incisively analyses, from a theoretically informed perspective, crucial aspects of India's journey from partial divestiture to privatisation, accompanied by case studies of enterprises being privatised in FY 2022.

Naib begins with the economic role of the state followed by theoretical and empirical evidence on the state versus private ownership in the first two chapters. Next, an overview of public sector in India including the New Public Sector Enterprise Policy for Atmanirbhar Bharat-2021 is discussed, before a broader examination of the global experience with privatisation is done. Naib then goes on to explore India's journey from partial divestiture to privatisation from 1991 to 2021 in four time slots based on the political party in power. The book also looks at big ticket privatisation and asset monetisation proposed in FY 2022. Many criticised the design of National Monetisation Plan as it may lead to concentration of wealth, increasing inequalities, asset stripping, and consumers paying higher charges. The book closes by presenting six instances of big-ticket privatisations ranging from airlines, airports, banks, insurance, as well as industries such as petroleum and telecoms.

The book's timely data and analysis of key developments will interest researchers in the fields of divestiture and privatisation in India.

Sudhir Naib, former Director and Emeritus Professor, Bharatiya Vidya Bhawan's Usha & Lakshmi Mittal Institute of Management, New Delhi, has authored three books published by Oxford University Press and Sage. He has authored research articles in *Economic & Political Weekly*, and many case studies published in Ivey Publishing, Emerald Emerging Markets Case Studies, *Asian Journal of Management Cases*, Case Centre, and India Case Research Centre.

Routledge Focus on Business and Management

The fields of business and management have grown exponentially as areas of research and education. This growth presents challenges for readers trying to keep up with the latest important insights. *Routledge Focus on Business and Management* presents small books on big topics and how they intersect with the world of business research.

Individually, each title in the series provides coverage of a key academic topic, whilst collectively, the series forms a comprehensive collection across the business disciplines.

Corporate Governance Models
A Critical Assessment
Marco Mastrodascio

Continuous Improvement Practice in Local Government
Insights from Australia and New Zealand
Matthew Pepper, Oriana Price and Arun Elias

Informal Leadership, Strategy and Organizational Change
The Power of Silent Authority
Dr. Brenetia J. Adams-Robinson

South African Business in China
Navigating Institutions
Dr. Kelly Meng

Privatisation in India
Journey and Challenges
Sudhir Naib

For more information about this series, please visit: www.routledge.com/ Routledge-Focus-on-Business-and-Management/book-series/FBM

Privatisation in India
Journey and Challenges

Sudhir Naib

Routledge
Taylor & Francis Group

LONDON AND NEW YORK

First published 2022
by Routledge
4 Park Square, Milton Park, Abingdon, Oxon OX14 4RN

and by Routledge
605 Third Avenue, New York, NY 10158

Routledge is an imprint of the Taylor & Francis Group, an informa business

British Library Cataloguing-in-Publication Data
A catalogue record for this book is available from the British Library

Library of Congress Cataloging-in-Publication Data
Names: Naib, Sudhir, author.
Title: Privatisation in India : journey and challenges / Sudhir Naib.
Description: Abingdon, Oxon ; New York, NY : Routledge, 2022. |
Series: Routledge focus on business & management |
Includes bibliographical references and index.
Identifiers: LCCN 2021049161 (print) | LCCN 2021049162 (ebook) |
ISBN 9781032201016 (hbk) | ISBN 9781032201030 (pbk) |
ISBN 9781003262213 (ebk)
Subjects: LCSH: Privatization–India. | Government business enterprises–India.
Classification: LCC HD4293.N328 2022 (print) |
LCC HD4293 (ebook) | DDC 338.954–dc23/eng/20211208
LC record available at https://lccn.loc.gov/2021049161
LC ebook record available at https://lccn.loc.gov/2021049162

ISBN: 978-1-03-220101-6 (hbk)
ISBN: 978-1-03-220103-0 (pbk)
ISBN: 978-1-00-326221-3 (ebk)

DOI: 10.4324/9781003262213

Typeset in Times New Roman
by Newgen Publishing UK

Dedicated to the memory of my parents Wazir Chand and Asha Rani for showing me that anything is possible with faith, hard work, and determination. A special thanks to my sister Vishu Bhalla, and my children Anuj, Priyanka, Parul for their continued support and encouragement.

Contents

Tables

Abbreviations

AAI	Airports Authority of India
AAHL	Adani Airport Holdings Limited
AI	Air India
AERA	Airports Economic Regulatory Authority
AISAM	Air India Specific Alternative Mechanism
AISATS	Air India Singapore Airport Terminal Services
BAA	British Airports Authority
BALCO	Bharat Aluminium Company Limited
BDL	Bharat Dynamics Limited
BEL	Bharat Electronics Limited
BIAL	Bangalore International Airport Limited
BJP	Bharatiya Janta Party
BPCL	Bharat Petroleum Corporation Limited
BSE	Bombay Stock Exchange
BSNL	Bharat Sanchar Nigam Limited
DFI	Development Finance Institution
DIAL	Delhi International Airport Limited
DIPAM	Department of Investment and Public Asset Management
DOT	Department of Telecom
EGOS	Empowered Group of Secretaries
EOI	Expression of Interest
ETFs	Exchange Traded Funds
FDI	Foreign Direct Investment
FM	Finance Minister
FPO	Follow on Public Offer
FY	Financial Year (April to March)
GDP	Gross Domestic Product
GoI	Government of India
GOM	Group of Ministers
HAL	Hindustan Aeronautics Limited

HPCL	Hindustan Petroleum Corporation Limited
HTL	Hindustan Teleprinters Limited
HUL	Hindustan Unilever Limited
HZL	Hindustan Zinc Limited
IAAI	International Airports Authority of India
IMF	International Monetary Fund
InvIT	Infrastructure Investment Trust
IOCL	Indian Oil Corporation Limited
IPCL	Indian Petrochemicals Corporation Limited
IPO	Initial Public Offer
IRDAI	Insurance Regulatory and Development Authority
ITDC	India Tourism Development Corporation
IWG	Internal Working Group
LIC	Life Insurance Corporation
M-cap	Market Capitalisation
MFIL	Modern Foods India Limited
MIAL	Mumbai International Airport Limited
MOUs	Memorandum of Understandings
MSMEs	Micro Small and Medium Enterprises
MTNL	Mahanagar Telephone Nigam Limited
NAA	National Airports Authority
NACIL	National Aviation Company of India Limited
NALCO	National Aluminium Company Limited
NARCL	National Asset Reconstruction Company Ltd
NBFCs	Non-banking Financial Companies
NDA	National Democratic Alliance
NHAI	National Highways Authority of India
NIP	National Infrastructure Pipeline
NITI	National Institution for Transforming India
NMP	National Monetisation Pipeline
NOIDA	New Okhla Industrial Development Authority
NRL	Numaligarh Refinery Limited
NSO	National Statistical Office
NYT	*The New York Times*
OECD	Organisation for Economic Co-operation and Development
OMDA	Operation Management Development Agreement
PIM	Preliminary Information Memorandum
PPP	Public Private Partnership
PPPAC	Public Private Partnership Appraisal Committee
PSEs	Public Sector Enterprises
PSU	Public Sector Undertakings

RBI	Reserve Bank of India
REITs	Real Estate Investment Trusts
SOEs	State Owned Enterprises
TDSAT	Telecom Dispute Settlement and Appellate Tribunal
TRAI	Telecom Regulatory Authority of India
UPA	United Progressive Alliance
UK	United Kingdom
US	United States
VRS	Voluntary Retirement Scheme
VSNL	Videsh Sanchar Nigam Limited
WHO	World Health Organisation

Introduction

Nationalisation and growth of public sector worldwide

There has been a long period characterised by nationalisation and growth in the size of the public sector worldwide. India also nationalised airlines, banks, insurance, coal, oil, and sick textile mills.

To improve SOEs performance, many countries undertook reform options, viz. divestiture (whereby private ownership is inducted in state-owned enterprises), greenfield privatisation (whereby the private sector is allowed to come and compete in areas hitherto reserved for the public sector), and cold privatisation (which grants greater autonomy to managers of state-owned enterprises through a memorandum of understanding).

Difference between disinvestment and privatisation

Before we go into the various issues relating to privatisation, we must clear one semantic problem. In India the term 'disinvestment' has been used, and the word 'privatisation' was avoided. What is the difference between disinvestment, and privatisation? Privatisation implies a change in ownership resulting in a change in management. Of late, the Indian government started using the term 'strategic disinvestment' where it ceded control to private buyers. Probably, for the first time, the government while presenting the federal budget for 2021–22, used the term 'privatisation', instead of 'strategic disinvestment'.

For the purpose of this book; we use the term privatisation as transfer of ownership and control of state-owned enterprises to the private sector. Disinvestment is dilution of state ownership but with control management still lying in the hands of the government. Thus, if share dilution is less than 51%, it is referred to as disinvestment, otherwise it is privatisation.

DOI: 10.4324/9781003262213-1

We use ₹ to denote Indian Rupee. In the Indian system of accounting a million is 10 lakhs, ten million is 1 crore, and a billion is 100 crore. The exchange rate of 1 USD was 74.27 Indian Rupee as on 17 November 2021.

India's recent major reforms driven by economic necessity

India's recent economic history has shown that major reforms have been driven by economic necessity. Earlier, it was the exceptionally severe balance of payments crisis in 1991 when a Congress led coalition government under Prime Minister P. V. Narasimha Rao took office on 21 June, and remained in office till 16 May 1996. In the previous 18 months, the country had gone through two unstable minority governments. Foreign exchange reserves had run down to $1.1 billion by the end of June 1991, barely enough for two weeks of imports. The immediate issue was India's struggle to avoid defaulting on loans on which it had never previously defaulted. India's foreign debt climbed to about $72 billion, making it the world's third largest debtor after Brazil and Mexico.[1]

The historic month of July 1991 also saw 47 tons of gold airlifted to London and pledged in Bank of England to raise $405 million to fund the current account deficit, the excess of imports over exports.[2] Earlier, the government had leased 20 tons of gold to State Bank of India to sell in international market. The Union budget was presented on 24 July, and earlier in the day the government tabled the Statement on Industrial Policy in the Parliament. This policy led to a much larger role for the private sector and openness to trade and foreign investment. The crisis paved the way for a much more market oriented economy. As of 3 September 2021, India's total foreign exchange reserve is US $642 billion (₹4,690,783 crore), of which Foreign currency assets are $580 billion, Gold $38 billion, SDRs $19 billion, and Reserve with IMF $5 billion).[3]

India went in for a big privatisation drive during the National Democratic Alliance government led by BJP under Prime Minister Atal Bihari Vajpayee (March 1998 to May 2004). However, for the next ten years under the United Progressive Alliance government led by Congress under Prime Minister Manmohan Singh (May 2004 to May 2014) only partial divestiture took place. The National Democratic Alliance government led by BJP under Prime Minister Narendra Damodardas Modi came to power in May 2014 and so in the subsequent general election in 2019.

In PM Modi's first term, only minority stakes in several government corporations were sold. Often Central Public Sector Enterprises

(CPSEs) with high reserves were asked to buy out the government's stock in other CPSEs. This balance sheet jugglery changed nothing in reality, but it cut the fiscal deficit. The Modi government attempted only one privatisation in 2018 – that of Air India – but so many conditions were attached to it that there were no bidders.

Emboldened by a decisive re-election that saw the BJP return with a full majority in Parliament for the second term in May 2019, the government set a target of taking the economy to USD 5 trillion over the next five years in 2024. India's GDP at the time was estimated at around USD 2.8 trillion.[4]

Slow down of economy in 2019

After demonetisation in November 2016, there was a slowdown in the economy and a rise in unemployment. While it seemed that things were looking better, the economy again slowed down in 2019.[5] The government introduced a large corporate tax cut in the hope of reviving investment, and the Reserve Bank of India, the central bank, carried out a series of policy rate reductions, a cumulative of 250 bps during February 2019 to May 2020 in the hope of reviving the economy.[6]

Privatisation push

On 20 November 2019, the government announced that full management control will be ceded to buyers of Bharat Petroleum Corporation Ltd (BPCL), Shipping Corporation of India (SCI) and Container Corporation of India Ltd (CONCOR). On 8 January 2020, strategic disinvestment was also approved for Minerals & Metals Trading Corporation Limited (MMTC), National Mineral Development Corporation (NMDC), MECON and Bharat Heavy Electricals Ltd (BHEL).[7]

Covid-19 pandemic

A once-in-a-century pandemic devastated most of the world's economies in 2020. Prime Minister Modi imposed a nationwide lockdown on the evening of 24 March 2020. The lockdown measures imposed to contain the spread of Covid-19 affected employment, business, trade, manufacturing, and services activities. An estimated 122 million workers found themselves without jobs in the ensuing lockdown. According to BBC News, of these 122 million, 91.3 millions were small traders and labourers. Also, salaried workers (17.8 million) and self-employed people (18.2 million) also lost work.[8]

New public sector enterprises policy for Atmanirbhar Bharat

The new public sector enterprises policy for Atmanirbhar Bharat (Self Reliant India) was announced by the Finance Minister Nirmala Sitharaman, in the budget speech on 1 February 2021. According to it, the commercial enterprises would be classified into Strategic and Non-strategic sectors. There would be bare minimum presence of the public sector enterprises in the four defined strategic areas, and the remaining CPSEs in the strategic sector would be privatised or merged or subsidiarised with other CPSEs or closed. In non-strategic sectors, CPSEs would be privatized; otherwise they would be closed.[9]

The Department of Investment and Public Asset Management (DIPAM) issued details of the New Public Sector Enterprise Policy for Atmanirbhar Bharat on 4 February 2021. Except for a few, all the Central Public Sector Enterprises would come into the ambit of privatisation. The PSEs in the nature of development and regulatory authorities, autonomous organisations, trusts, development financing/refinancing institutions, some of which have been created through Acts of Parliament, would be outside the purview of the new policy.[10]

The FM in her budget speech stated that disinvestments/privatisations which could not be completed in 2020–21 namely BPCL, Air India, Shipping Corporation of India, Container Corporation of India, IDBI Bank, BEML, Pawan Hans, Neelachal Ispat Nigam limited among others were now slated for Fiscal 2022, i.e. the Financial Year 2021–22. Also, privatisation of two public sector banks other than IDBI Bank, and one general insurance company would be undertaken in the year 2021–22. The government would also bring the IPO of Life Insurance Corporation (LIC) hitherto untouched all these years of disinvestment.[11]

The detailed plan for National Monetisation Pipeline (NMP) was announced on 23 August 2021, which was earlier proposed in the union budget speech. The government is looking to monetise assets (other than lands) of about ₹ 6 trillion (i.e.₹ 6 lakh crore) over four years ending 2024–25. The plan covers 20 asset classes spread over 12 line ministries and departments. The top three sectors by value are roads (₹ 1.6 trillion), railways (₹1.5 trillion) and power (₹ 85,032 crore). It was clarified that the ownership of all these assets would remain with the government and there would be a mandatory hand-back of assets after a certain time period. 'So, the government is not selling away these assets,' the FM said.[12]

Other than opposition parties, many criticised the design of NMP as it would lead to monopoly/duopoly/oligopoly with all its attendant problems – concentration of wealth, increasing inequalities, asset stripping, and consumers paying higher charges. The government is also planning to sell public sector undertaking land parcels and unlike NMP, ownership would change.

Post Covid response

The Organisation for Economic Co-operation and Development (OECD), an international organisation of 38 member countries which span the globe, from North and South America to Europe and Asia-Pacific, reported in June 2020 that governments are considering taking equity stakes or may be considering whether to do so in distressed firms among the crisis-response tools. The OECD report estimated that the Covid-19 pandemic may, therefore, result in increased state ownership or control of enterprises. Such interventions tend to target companies, whose failure could pose a strain on the economy, for example by increasing unemployment, interrupting essential transport connections, jeopardising the provision of crucial services or products, or obstructing access to finance. [13]

The *Guardian*, London, wrote on 19 October 2020 that Covid-19 has exposed the catastrophic impact of privatising vital services. It wrote, that the pandemic revealed that there are goods and services that must be placed outside the laws of market.[14] However, the Indian government was pushing hard on the pedal of privatisation.

The book

The purpose of writing this book is to enable readers to make an informed judgment about privatisation of Central Public Sector Enterprises in India.

The Privatisation in India: Journey and Challenges is a comprehensive work which incisively analyses from a theoretically informed perspective crucial aspects of this topical issue through case studies of enterprises being privatised in FY 2022 (National Carrier Air India; the second largest oil marketing company in India BPCL; IPO of LIC – a corporation hitherto untouched all these years of disinvestment; privatisation of banks and airports; and the two top loss making enterprises in the Telecom sector – BSNL and MTNL).

Structure of the book

Chapter 1 deals with the economic role of the state. After independence, India nationalised airlines, banks, insurance, coal, oil, and sick textile mills. The argument for government ownership was on the assumption that government can use SOEs to correct for various types of market failures. But there are non-market failures also. The Government of India, Economic Survey 2019–20 stated that the Indian economy is replete with examples where government intervened, even if there was no risk of market failures, and in fact, in some instances its intervention created market failures.

In Chapter 2 – 'Does ownership matter?' – both theoretical and empirical evidence is analysed for and against each form of ownership, that is, public and private. It then examines the political agency problem in India. In the last section, we examine the distributional impact of privatisation.

Chapter 3 looks closely at the public sector in India. First an overview of what constitutes public sector, departmental, and non-departmental enterprises, and government companies, is dealt with. Then we look at India's industrial policy. Performance of Central Public Sector Enterprises (CPSEs) is examined next. The chapter concludes with the shift in government policy on public sector with the announcement of the New Public Sector Enterprise Policy for Atmanirbhar Bharat, 2021.

An overview of global experience with privatisation is given in Chapter 4. The progress of privatisation is analysed in the 1980s, 1990s, 2000s, and from 2009 onwards.

Chapter 5 deals with India's journey from partial divestiture to privatisation from 1991 to 2021. It starts with analysing the triggers for disinvestment in 1991, which we argue was mainly fiscal distress and conditions put in by IMF for giving loans to India. Next we look into politics of disinvestment. We argue that to take politically risky decision to privatise depends on the ideology of the ruling political party and in a coalition government bringing all on the same platform is crucial. Broadly the Congress led governments' resorted to partial disinvestment of CPSEs, while the BJP led governments pursued strategic disinvestment leading to management transfer to the private entity. Since the initiation of the disinvestment process in 1991–92, the policy has evolved depending on the ideology of the ruling party at the Union level. The journey of divestiture is covered in four broad time slots. The first phase from 1991–92 to 1997–98 under Congress led United Progressive Alliance (UPA) government, and later Congress supported the United Front Government. The second phase from 1998–99 to

2003–04 under National Democratic Alliance (NDA) government led by Bharatiya Janta Party (BJP). The third phase from 2004–05 to 2013–14, under UPA government led by Congress party, and the fourth phase from 2014–15 onwards under the NDA government led by BJP.

Next, Chapter 6 looks at the big ticket privatisation and asset monetisation proposed in the Fiscal 2022. India's ambitious plan to generate revenue of ₹ 1.75 lakh crore from privatisation/disinvestment of CPSEs in Fiscal 2022 is discussed along with criteria for selection of SOEs for privatisation. Further, we discuss the three pronged government strategy for raising resources to finance new infrastructure investments. The salient features of the National Monetisation Pipeline announced in August 2021 are discussed. Efficiency scrutiny of government funded organisations is suggested to optimise resources.

In the next six chapters we discuss the big ticket privatisations which government is focusing on either to get money or stop losing further money – the top three loss making CPSEs (Air India, BSNL, & MTNL), Maharatna BPCL listed in the top ten profit making CPSEs, and privatising airports, public sector banks, and disinvestment in LIC.

Chapter 7 looks closely at the privatisation of Air India, both in terms of past efforts and the present. Finally, Tata Sons won the bid to acquire the Air India and is likely to take control and operate the Airlines from early 2022. It analyses how the terms of sale have undergone changes.

The oil sector has been considered a strategic sector and privatising a profitable CPSE having a ranking in global Fortune 500 companies is dealt with in Chapter 8. It looks at privatisation of Bharat Petroleum Corporation Limited for which the government invited bids for the sale of its entire 52.98% stake in March 2020. Ahead of privatisation, BPCL decided to offer Voluntary Retirement and also the FDI limit was increased from 49% to 100%. The last date to submit EOI had to be extended multiple times and finally it closed on 16 November 2020, a year after the announcement.

Chapter 9 looks into airport privatisation from a global and Indian perspective. Airport operations in India and privatisation of airports are described. The recent privatisation of airports in 2019 and 2020 is looked at, along with the associated controversies. The proposed monetisation of airports in 2021–22 is examined along with the impact of the Covid pandemic.

Chapter 10 looks at privatisation of banks. It deals with why banks are unique institutions and unlike any other public sector enterprise privatisation, it needs special consideration. Next we give the story of nationalisation of banks which took place on 19 July 1969. This is followed by the policy on privatisation of banks as given in the Union budget for Fiscal 2022. Later, we discuss the much debated recommendations of the Reserve Bank of India's Internal Working Group (IWG) to allow large corporate/industrial houses as promoters of banks.

Chapter 11 looks closely at the proposed IPO of Life Insurance Corporation (LIC), and the privatisation of one general insurance company. We also look at global insurance sector and India's place in it.

In Chapter 12, we deal with BSNL & MTNL in the telecommunication sector. Among the top ten loss making CPSEs from past few years, Bharat Sanchar Nigam Limited (BSNL), Mahanagar Telephone Nigam Limited (MTNL), and Air India have the ignominy to occupy the top three positions. We deal with Government's earlier plans to revive BSNL and MTNL, and their merger. This is followed by the Government's current proposal of asset monetisation in the two CPSEs.

References

1. Bernard Weinraub, 'Economic crisis forcing once self-reliant India to seek aid', *The New York Times*, 29 June 1991, www.nytimes.com/1991/06/29/world/economic-crisis-forcing-once-self-reliant-india-to-seek-aid.html
2. Gayatri Nayak, 'When 47 tonnes of gold was in the middle of the road', *The Economic Times*, 5 July 2017, accessed 2 July 2021, https://economictimes.indiatimes.com/news/economy/finance/when-47-tonnes-of-gold-was-in-the-middle-of-road/articleshow/59447917.cms
3. Reserve Bank of India, Weekly Statistical Supplement, 10 September 2021, https://rbidocs.rbi.org.in/rdocs/Wss/PDFs/2T_100920217137A0FF319A401AB74C876B3F4AB841.PDF
4. The Economic Times, 'Modi govt's USD 5-trillion GDP target by 2024 looks unimaginably ambitious', 12 January 2020, https://economictimes.indiatimes.com/news/economy/policy/modi-govts-usd-5-trillion-gdp-target-by-2024-looks-unimaginably-ambitious/articleshow/73212751.cms?from=mdr
5. Arvind Subramanian and Josh Felman, Harvard Kennedy School, CID Faculty Working Paper No. 370, December 2019 'India's great slowdown: What happened? What's the way out?', www.hks.harvard.edu/sites/default/files/centers/cid/files/publications/faculty-working-papers/2019-12-cid-wp-369-indian-growth-diagnosis-remedies-final.pdf
6. Reserve Bank of India, Annual Report, 2020-21, p. 7. https://rbidocs.rbi.org.in/rdocs/AnnualReport/PDFs/0RBIAR202021_F49F9833694E84C16AAD01BE48F53F6A2.PDF
7. PIB, Cabinet Committee on Economic Affairs, 'Cabinet approves strategic disinvestment of CPSEs', 20 November 2019. https://pib.gov.in/PressReleasePage.aspx?PRID=1592540, and PIB, 'Cabinet approves 'In Principle' strategic disinvestment of equity shareholding of Minerals &

Metals Trading Corporation Limited, National Mineral Development Corporation, MECON and Bharat Heavy Electricals Ltd in Neelachal Ispat Nigam Limited. a JV Company with two Government of Odisha State PSUs', 8 January 2020, https://pib.gov.in/Pressreleaseshare.aspx?PRID= 1598715

8. Nikhil Inamdar, 'Coronavirus lockdown: India jobless numbers cross 120 million in April 2020', 6 May 2020, BBC News, Mumbai. www.bbc. com/news/world-asia-india-52559324

9. Government of India, Budget 2021–2022, Speech of Nirmala I. Sitharaman, Minister of Finance, 1 February 2021, www.indiabudget. gov.in/doc/budget_speech.pdf and PIB, Government of India, 1 February 2021, https://pib.gov.in/PressReleseDetailm.aspx?PRID=1693899

10. Department of Investment and Public Asset Management (DIPAM), 'New Public Sector Enterprise Policy for Atmanirbhar Bharat', Office Memorandum, 4 February 2021.

11. Government of India, Budget 2021–2022, Speech of Nirmala I. Sitharaman, Minister of Finance, 1 February 2021, www.indiabudget. gov.in/doc/budget_speech.pdf, and PIB, Government of India, 1 February 2021, https://pib.gov.in/PressReleseDetailm.aspx?PRID=1693899

12. Nikunj Ohri and Indivjal Dhasmana, 'FM announces plan to monetise assets, realise Rs 6 trillion till 2024–25', *Business Standard*, New Delhi, 23 August 2021 www.business-standard.com/article/economy-policy/fm-announces-plan-to-monetise-assets-realise-rs-6-trillion-till-2024-25-121082300923_1.html

13. OECD, 'The Covid-19 crisis and state ownership in the economy: Issues and policy considerations', 25 June 2020, www.oecd.org/coronavirus/policy-responses/the-covid-19-crisis-and-state-ownership-in-the-economy-issues-and-policy-considerations-ce417c46/

14. The Guardian, 'The Covid-19 has exposed the catastrophic impact of privatising vital services', 19 October 2020, www.theguardian.com/society/2020/oct/19/covid-19-exposed-catastrophic-impact-privatising-vital-services

1 The economic role of the state

Expansion in state owned enterprises (SOEs)

The dominant view in the literature on development economics in the 1950s and 1960s was that the government had an important role to play and that it should undertake activities that would compensate for 'market failure'. The argument for government ownership rested primarily on the assumption that government can use SOEs to correct for various types of market failure.

There was a long period characterised by nationalisation and growth in the size of the public sector worldwide. These nationalisations took place practically in every area of economic activity in a majority of countries.

In industrialised nations, state ownership was viewed as the remedy for market failures such as externalities and monopoly, which at that time was considered widespread. In developing nations these justifications were coupled with arguments that SOEs facilitated economic independence and planned development. There was thus a clear trend towards greater reliance on public ownership until the final quarter of the twentieth century.

State-owned enterprises (SOEs) accounted for 20% of investment, 5% of employment, and up to 40% of domestic output in countries around the world [Asian Development Bank (2020)].[1]

Nationalisation of airlines, banks, insurance, coal, oil, and sick textile mills in India

Indian National Congress had uninterrupted rule in India after independence in 1947 to 1977. Jawaharlal Nehru, the first Prime Minister of independent India who remained in office from 1947 till 1964, was deeply influenced by the centralised planned economy model of Soviets based on state ownership of the means of production and distribution.

DOI: 10.4324/9781003262213-2

Later, his daughter Indira Gandhi was the Prime Minister from 1966 to 1977, and from 1980 to Oct 1984. During the prime ministership of Nehru and Indira Gandhi, India nationalised airlines, banks, insurance, coal, oil, and sick textile mills (Observer Research Foundation (2018)).[2]

Airlines. India nationalised nine airlines in 1953 and replaced them with Indian Airlines and Air India International.

Banks. In 1955, it nationalised the largest bank in the country Imperial Bank of India and State Bank of India came into being. In 1969, Indira Gandhi nationalised 14 largest private banks of the country. With Imperial Bank already nationalised and renamed as State Bank of India in 1955, this decision made 80% of banking assets under the control of State.

Insurance. The government nationalised 154 Indian, 16 non-Indian insurers, and 75 provident societies into a single entity and Life Insurance Corporation (LIC) was created in 1956. In 1972, general insurance business of 55 Indian companies, 52 foreign insurers were amalgamated into four companies – National Insurance, Oriental Insurance, New India Assurance, and United India Insurance.

Coal. In 1972, 937 coal mines, 226 coking coal mines, and 711 non-coking coal mines were nationalised and Coal India as a holding company was formed.

Oil. At the time of India's independence, there were three foreign oil companies: Esso, Burmah Shell, and Caltex. All three were nationalised during 1974–76 and Indian Oil Corporation, Bharat Petroleum Corporation, and Hindustan Petroleum Corporation came into being.

Sick textile mills. 103 sick textile mills were nationalised and transferred to National Textile Corporation through Sick Textile Undertakings (Nationalisation Act 1974).

Market failures

According to Stieglitz, (1986) there are eight principal sources of market failures, each of which has been used to justify the possibility of government activity in the market place.[3] The first six (natural monopoly, public goods, externalities, incomplete markets, information failures, unemployment) describe circumstances under which the market may not be Pareto efficient. Pareto efficiency is when an economy has its resources and goods allocated to the maximum level of efficiency and no change can be made without making someone worse off.

The last two (income distribution, and merit goods) describe situations where government intervention may be justified even if the economy is Pareto efficient.

The following description of principal sources of market and non-market failures is an updated version of originally published in *Disinvestment in India: Policies, Procedures, Practices*, pp. 43–7. Copyright 2004 © Sudhir Naib. All rights reserved. Reproduced with the permission of the copyright holder and the publishers, SAGE Publications India Pvt Ltd, New Delhi.

Natural monopoly

In some industries there are relatively few firms. This suggests absence of strong competition. However, the presence of only a few firms in itself does not necessarily imply that the firms are not acting competitively. If there are a large number of potential entrants, the existing firms may not be able to exercise monopoly power. In other instances, there are barriers to entry arising from what economists refer to as increasing returns to scale.

Those are referred to as natural monopolies, where the costs of production – per unit output, decline with the scale of production. Under certain circumstances it may be more efficient to have one firm producing than many. Monopolies are generally viewed as bad. The reason for that is if unregulated, monopolies – whether natural or not, will restrict output to attain a higher price.

Public goods

There are some goods that either will not be supplied by the market or, if supplied, will be supplied in an insufficient quantity. These are called pure public goods. They have two critical properties. First, it does not cost anything for an additional individual to enjoy the benefits of the public goods i.e. there is zero marginal cost for the additional individual enjoying the good. Second, it is, in general, difficult or impossible to exclude individuals from the enjoyment of the public good. Examples of such type of goods is provisioning of clean air and defence. The fact that a private market will not supply, or will supply too little, of public goods provides a rationale for many government activities.

Externalities

There are many cases where the actions of one firm imposes a cost on other firms but does not compensate them (negative externalities), or alternatively, where one firm confers a benefit on other firms but does not get rewarded for it (positive externalities). An example of negative externality is air and water pollution. Poor air quality in Delhi due to stubble burning after harvest in northern Indian states is an example. Since individuals do not bear the full cost of the negative externalities they generate, they will engage in an excessive amount of such activities. Conversely, since individuals do not enjoy the full benefits of activities generating positive externalities, they will engage in too little of these. In such cases, there is a rationale for government intervention through appropriate tax-subsidy policies to compensate for the market's tendency towards either excessive production or underproduction.

The scientists of the Intergovernmental Panel on Climate Change (IPCC), a United Nations body, reported in August 2021 that global warming is dangerously close to spiralling out of control. The deadly heat waves, gargantuan hurricanes, and other weather extremes that are already happening will only become worse. The UN Secretary General, António Guterres, said that 'this report must sound a death knell for coal and fossil fuels, before they destroy our planet'.[4] The governments have to intervene when code red has been sounded for humanity.

Incomplete markets

Pure public goods and services are not the only goods or services that private markets fail to provide adequately. Whenever private markets fail to provide a good or service, even though the cost of providing it is less than what individuals are willing to pay, there is a market failure. This is referred to as incomplete markets (a complete market would provide all goods and services for which the cost of provision is less than what individuals are willing to pay). Examples of such cases are particularly in providing insurance and credit. Also, in many cases, large-scale coordination is required to generate market, and this may require government intervention.

Information failures

A number of government activities are motivated by imperfect information on the part of consumers, and the belief that the market, by itself, will supply too little information. Information asymmetry is likely to lead to allocative inefficiency, for example, in case of goods/investment actions, whose quality and consequences are known after long experience, and it is often too late to undo the adverse consequences of their use or neglect. Regulatory bodies in many sectors are to check this.

Unemployment

Many economists take the view that high levels of unemployment are evidence that something is not working well in the market and is a symptom of market failure.

The preceding six sources of market failure would result in the economy being inefficient in the absence of government intervention – that is, the market economy if left to itself would not be Pareto optimal. But, even if the economy were Pareto optimal, there are two further arguments for government intervention. These are income distribution, and provisioning of merit goods.

Income distribution

Competitive market may give rise to a very unequal distribution of income. One of the important activities of the government is to redistribute income. However, equality and productivity become competitive values beyond a certain point for two reasons. First, there is an adverse incentive effect of progressive taxation on initiative, risk taking, and enterprise development. Second, there is also an adverse incentive effect of receiving income without expanding effort. Here lies the problem for any government – how much more equality do we want in terms of sacrifice in productivity?

Merit goods

Goods that the government compels individuals to consume are called merit goods. An example of such goods would be providing education, preventing smoking, etc. Underlying this concept is the 'paternalistic' role of the government. Here the belief is that government should intervene in cases, where individuals seemingly do not do what is in their own best interest and the kind of intervention that is required must be stronger than a simple provision of information. Providing toilet to every household is an example of merit good.

Now, policy makers increasingly use 'nudges', a concept popularised by Richard H. Thaler and Cass R. Sunstein (2009) in their book *Nudge* to alter people behaviour.[5] A nudge is any aspect of the choice architecture (the context in which people make decisions) that alters people's behaviour in a predictable way without forbidding any options or significantly changing their economic incentives. The Indian government used nudges to prevent open defecation, and in overcoming Covid-19 vaccine hesitancy.

Government (non-market) failures

Detecting the presence of market failure is easy but the task of pre-scribing curative policy interventions is indeed complicated. Faced with market failure in a sector, the dilemma is often sought to be resolved through direct entry of government in the production/provision of goods and services produced by such a sector. However, administrative costs and harmful side effects of policy interventions are often difficult to fathom in advance.

The government (non-market) failures are however not less ram-pant than the market failure. As no individual or group owns a state enterprise, no one has a clear stake in SOE returns. Politicians, bureaucrats, employees, and other interest groups often thrust mul-tiple and often conflicting goals upon SOEs (e.g., profit maximisation, employment maximisation, and a host of other social objectives). Simultaneously, numbers of constraints (e.g., restricting layoffs, price increases, and choice of suppliers or markets) are imposed. Multiple objectives and multiple constraints increase transaction costs, distort the incentives facing SOE managers, and reduce managerial effort. Further, as SOEs have access to subsidies, transfers, government guaranteed loans; there is no threat of bankruptcy to act as a check on inefficiency. Following are the two major types of non-market failures.

Internalities / private goals

Public agencies develop their own standards/goals to guide, regulate, and evaluate their performance. These are called 'internalities' / 'private goals'. Non-market agencies often develop internalities that do not bear a close connection with the public purpose for which they were set up. Also the incentive to control costs in public agencies is weak because of lack of competition in many sectors. Specific internalities that often accompany non-market activities and leads to non-market failure are growth in budget (the more the better), ambiguity and multiplicity of objectives. Multiple objectives and multiple constraints increase trans-action costs, distort the incentives for managers and reduce managerial effort.

Distributional Inequities

The government in carrying out its activities either of direct produc-tion of public goods or of regulating the industry has to place power in the hands of some to be exercised over others. This redistribution of power provides opportunities for inequity and abuse by giving rise to 'rent-seeking'. Krueger (1974) stated that heavy reliance on a variety of controls to direct economic activity in the desired channels led to 'rent-seeking'.[6] Public policies generate economic rent for those groups or individuals favoured by the policies. Examples include permits/licences, and subsidies. Many studies have brought out that subsidies do not reach the targeted groups. Price subsidies to infrastructure almost always benefit the non-poor disproportionately (World Bank, 1994).[7]

Revisiting government role in economy

What were thought to be stable assumptions about the role of government in governance were unsettled by wave of privatisation. The main thrust of privatisation initially began from the UK's Margaret Thatcher and John Major's Conservative governments (1979–1997). Large privatisations took place in much of Western Europe, Latin America, parts of Asia, and, perhaps most dramatically, in the former USSR and its former Eastern Europe socialist allies. These privatisations were justified in different ways in different places and at different times, but often references were made to freeing enterprise, reducing tax rates, improving the quality and efficiency of services, raising public revenue, decreasing debt, and spreading shareholder wealth.

Further, many SOEs performed poorly incurring high financial and economic costs. In many countries SOEs were becoming a fiscal burden and a source of fiscal risk as they weaken the financial system. Continued lending to unprofitable companies can create contingent liabilities and is likely to destabilise the macro economy.

The Government of India, Ministry of Finance, Economic Survey for the year 2019–20, stated that while there is a case for government intervention when markets do not function properly, excessive intervention, especially when markets can do the job of enhancing citizens' welfare perfectly well, stifles economic freedom.[8]

The Economic Survey further went on to say that Indian economy is replete with examples where government intervened even if there was no risk of market failure, and in fact, in some instances its intervention had created market failures. The Survey attributed this partly due to the legacy of post-independence economic policies which the country followed. It concluded that the role of markets has been recognised globally, it is only natural that markets are allowed to work to enable quick wealth creation and thereby economic growth. This was probably the precursor to privatisation of SOEs in the coming year.

In the India's union/federal government budget for the fiscal 2022, many steps towards undoing crucial parts of the earlier legacy of nationalisation of private companies were taken. It was announced that two of the state-owned banks would be privatised. Also an increase in the cap on foreign direct investment in insurance companies from 49% to 74% was announced. The budget outlined plans to set up an asset reconstruction company, or 'bad bank', to clean up lenders by buying bad assets and selling them to specialised investors.

However, a group of economists believed that public sector provides the much-needed shock absorber in an economy that might experience turbulences like inflation, depression, unemployment, and other temporary disturbances in a market economy.[9]

The Covid-19 pandemic has been witnessing two contradictory economic phenomena: continuing privatisation and monetisation of state assets by some government's like India, while some governments like OECD countries are considering taking equity stakes in distressed firms.

References

1. Asian Development Bank (2020), *Reforms, Opportunities, and Challenges for State-Owaned Enterprises*, edited by Edimon Ginting and Kaukab Naqvi: Preface, xii–xiii www.adb.org/sites/default/files/publication/618761/reforms-opportunities-challenges-state-owned-enterprises.pdf
2. Observer Research Foundation (2018), '70 policies that shaped India: 1947 to 2017', Gautam Chikermane.
3. Stiglitz, J. E. (1986), *Economics of the Public Sector*. New York: WW Norton & Company.
4. Nina Chestney and Andrea Januta, 'UN climate change report sounds "code red for humanity",' Reuters, 9 August 2021, www.reuters.com/business/environment/un-sounds-clarion-call-over-irreversible-climate-impacts-by-humans-2021-08-09/
5. Richard H. Taler and Carl R. Sustein. (2009). *Nudge: Improving Decisions about Health, Wealth, and Happiness* (New Delhi, Penguin Books India Pvt Ltd).
6. Krueger, A. O. (1974), 'The political economy of the rent-seeking society', *The American Economic Review 64*(3): 291–303.
7. World Bank (1994). *World Development Report, 1994*. New York: Oxford University Press.

8. Government of India, Ministry of Finance, *Economic Survey, 2019–20*, Volume 1 Chapter 4, 'Undermining markets: when government intervention hurts more than it helps', pp. 67–99.
9. Chalam, K. S., 'Public sector is the lifeline of the marginalised', *The Tribune*, 9 March 2021. www.tribuneindia.com/news/comment/public-sector-is-the-lifeline-of-the-marginalised-222540

2   Does ownership matter?

Theoretical arguments favouring public and private ownership

There are theoretical arguments favouring each form of ownership that is public and private. The difference between public and private enterprises starts with the very objectives of the owners in the two cases. In private ownership, it is generally assumed that the motive of the owners is profit maximisation whereas in public ownership, the assumption is that the objective is to maximise social welfare. This leads to the *public interest theory of state-owned enterprise*. The public interest theory assumes that if monitoring of management is equally effective under both types of ownerships, public ownership has some potential advantages over private ownership as it allows the government to achieve distributional objectives, and provides it with additional policy instruments to correct any deviation between the social and private returns.

The owners of both public and private enterprise face a similar agency problem, that is, how can managers and other employees (the agents) be encouraged to act in ways that contribute maximally to the owners' (the principals') objectives? This is the problem of incentives or of enterprise monitoring.

The following description of agency problem including the political agency problem in India is based on *Disinvestment in India: Policies, Procedures, Practices*, pp. 29–32. Copyright 2004 © Sudhir Naib. Reproduced with the permission of the copyright holder and the publishers, SAGE Publications India Pvt Ltd, New Delhi.

The key hypothesis concerning the agency problem, at the enterprise level is that private ownership is associated with a more effective incentive structure than public ownership, that is, there will be less scope under private ownership for managers and workers to pursue their own objectives at the expense of owners.

DOI: 10.4324/9781003262213-3

The fundamental argument is that as residual claimants to firms' revenues, the owners have every incentive to act efficiently. Further, there exist several mechanisms such as signals from stock market, threat of takeover bids, and bankruptcy threat in the private sector which constrain agents to pursue their own objectives at the cost of the principals.

A common criticism of public ownership is that the monitoring of enterprises tends to be poor. In case of SOEs, the full monitoring hierarchy includes voters, elected political representatives, civil servants, and the managers of SOEs. This leads to a number of principal agent problems. The political agency problem associated with the relationships between voters and the political decision-makers is of particular significance. The politicians and or bureaucrats responsible for monitoring SOEs can themselves be viewed as agents of the wider public (the principals), and it is the welfare of public that is the ultimate benchmark against which performance should be judged. The incentives for politicians to act in the best interests of the wider public will depend upon factors such as the nature of the relevant political system and the closeness of impending elections. In practice, monitoring the performance of SOEs is likely to be just one of the responsibilities of the political decision maker. Further, performance of a SOE may not have any bearing on the electoral prospects, as election is concerned with a wide range of issues and not merely how an SOE is being run.

Also bureaucrats and politicians can introduce their own agendas into the process. Bureaucrats, for example, may pursue the goal of expanding their own departments while politicians will be concerned about their political careers and their individual and party electoral prospects. Bureaucratic agendas may, therefore, result in excessive monitoring and control over SOEs, while political agendas may introduce goals such as redistribution of resources to favoured interest groups (for example provision of high wages and secure employment to SOE workers) and exercise of patronage. This implies that the objectives of political decision makers can be expected to deviate significantly from social welfare objectives. Thus the political agency problem tends to weaken any general advantage that might be claimed for public enterprise on account of its preferred objectives. It tilts the balance of advantages towards private ownership, and weakens the case for state intervention.

As such there are four potential sources of sub-optimality in control of SOEs:

(a) Displacement of social objectives by political objectives which may lead to redundant costs and also rising costs.
(b) Political intervention in managerial decision.

(c) Private goals that lead to budget growth (more is better) and growth in employment.
(d) Internal inefficiencies in bureaucratic activity.

Political agency problem in India

It is interesting to note that after the tenth Lok Sabha election in 1991, India had eight parliamentary elections till 2019, and no political party has thrust SOEs reforms into electoral politics as a major issue. Instead, the electoral agenda has been dominated by secular versus religious politics, corruption, and personalities. This raises the question that why do economic reforms have such low electoral concern in India? The theoretical model of political agency problem explains this.

There are considerable informational asymmetries between politicians and voters in India. Due to low level of education, the masses have not shown interest in the various economic reforms barring those which affect them directly in short-run. Reforms which may impact large population adversely can be politically risky as opposition parties can mobilise public opinion against the government.

Political attractiveness of SOE reforms depends on its political costs and benefits. In a typical case, the political costs must be borne up-front in the form of antagonising labour unions, managers, suppliers, and other powerful beneficiaries of state ownership. In return, some political benefits may flow immediately, for example, receipts to the treasury, while others may materialise in later years in the form of better quality of products/services, or more supply for consumers, lower burdens on tax payers, attractive returns to investors, and so on.

The political attractiveness of SOE reforms depends on these costs and benefits as well as their time of distribution. For example, privatisation will be more attractive politically if the political benefits can be preponed and the political costs postponed. If all reforms are done at once, political costs of reform peak in the early years, while the benefits which may be uncertain are expected to flow in later years, making this a risky strategy for those in power. Such a risk may be worth taking only if there is an economic crisis.

It is in light of this, that the Government of India's policy announcements on public sector and asset monetisation coupled with big ticket privatisations due in Fiscal 2022 have to be watched with excitement.

Empirical evidence about ownership

When governments divested state-owned enterprises in developed economies, especially in the 1980s and 1990s, their objectives were usually to enhance economic efficiency by improving firm performance and increase its revenue, and to introduce competition in monopolised sectors (Vickers and Yarrow, 1988).[1]

The findings of empirical research on the effects of privatisation up to 2000 (mainly from developed and middle-income countries) have been brought together by Megginson and Netter (2001).[2]

Sheltered from competition, state enterprises were often overstaffed and required to set prices below costs, resulting in financial losses that in acute cases amounted to as much as 5–6% of gross domestic product (GDP) annually (Kikeri and Nellis (2004)).[3] To cover state enterprise losses through fiscal transfers, required governments to finance larger fiscal deficits and increase tax revenues, and or reduce public spending in other areas.

Measuring impact of privatisation

Generally, two empirical approaches have been used to measure the impact of privatisation on firms' post-privatisation performance and efficiency. The first is comparing the performance of government-owned firms to that of privately owned firms. The second approach consists of comparing pre-and post-divestment performance for companies privatised via share issues (public offerings).

However, there are a number of methodological problems like sample selection bias (for example, if the well performing firms are privatised first), data availability, and consistency in analysing the economic effects of privatisation.

Approach I: Comparing government-owned firms to privately-owned firms

Studies in this tradition compare post-privatisation performance changes with either a comparison group of non-privatised firms or with a counterfactual.

One of the first studies to compare SOE and private firm performance is that of Ehrlich et al. (1994). These authors used a sample of 23 comparable international airlines (18 from developed countries and five from developing/emerging countries) of different ownership categories over the period 1973–1983 for which they had data on cost and output for comparable goods. The authors find a significant association between ownership and firm-specific rates of productivity growth. The study also suggested that the benefits derive primarily from complete privatisation of the firm. Partial change from state to private ownership had little effect on long-run productivity growth.[4]

Other studies have employed a similar approach examining differences in efficiency between private and government-owned firms within a specific country, such as Majumdar (1996) for Indian firms and Tian (2000) for Chinese firms. Both authors find that private sector firms are more efficient.[5,6]

Naib (2004) studied the effect of ownership, competition, and efficiency in the Indian context and concluded that at the enterprise level, there is little empirical justification for a general presumption in favour of either type of ownership. Further, the empirical study results indicated that more than ownership it is the degree of competition that affects the performance of an enterprise.[7]

Among studies using a counterfactual approach, one often cited study is the World Bank sponsored study by Galal et al. (1994). The authors compared the actual post-privatisation performance of 12 large firms in the airlines and utilities industry in Britain, Chile, Malaysia, and Mexico to a counterfactual performance. The study found net welfare gains in 11 of the 12 cases considered.[8]

In a cross-country, multi-industry comparisons of private and government-owned firms, Boardman and Vining (1989) use measures of X-efficiency and profitability ratios of the 500 largest non-US manufacturing and mining corporations in 1983 ('The International 500'; Fortune, 1983). Privately owned firms were found to be significantly more profitable and productive than state-owned and mixed ownership enterprises were no more profitable than SOEs.[9]

Another study by Frydman et al. (1999), which compared the performance of privatised and state firms in the transition economies of Central Europe in 1994 and found that privatised firms perform better than the state-owned firms.[10]

Dinc and Gupta (2011) examined the influence of political and financial factors on the decision to privatise government-owned firms in India using data from the 1990–2004 periods. They found that profitable firms and firms with a lower wage bill are likely to be privatised early and that the government delays privatisation in regions where the governing party faces more competition from opposition parties. The results therefore suggest that firms' financial characteristics have a significant impact on the government's decision to privatise. This raises an identification issue for evaluating the effect of privatisation on firm performance: if more profitable firms are more likely to be privatised, we may overstate the impact of privatisation on profitability when we compare the performance of government-owned to that of privatised firms. The authors after addressing the selection bias, found that privatisation still has a positive impact on performance in India.[11]

Government of India, Economic Survey 2019–20, analysed the before–after performance of 11 CPSEs that had undergone strategic disinvestment from 1999–2000 to 2003–04. These CPSEs were compared with their peers in the same industry group. The analysis showed that these privatised CPSEs, on an average, performed better post privatisation than their peers. The Economic Survey concluded that disinvestment improves firm performance, overall productivity, and unlocks enterprises potential to create wealth. It recommended aggressive disinvestment preferably through the route of strategic sale to bring in higher profitability, promote efficiency, increase competitiveness, and to promote professionalism in management in CPSEs.[12] But there are a number of methodological issues in such comparisons.

Approach II: Comparing pre-and post-divestment performance for companies privatised by public share offerings

The first study using this methodology was by Megginson, Nash, and van Randenborgh (1994). The results showed significant improvement in company performance, post-privatisation.[13] Megginson and Netter (2001) note that this methodology suffers from several drawbacks. However, it allows analysis of large samples of firms from different industries, countries, and time periods.[14]

Li et al. (2016) used a database of 204 Chinese SIPs from 1999 to 2009 matched with otherwise comparable state-owned enterprises and privately-owned firms. The authors found a significant positive increase in profitability post-SIP in divested Chinese state-owned companies.[15]

Impact of partial privatisation on firm performance

Since management control is not transferred to private owners it is widely contended that partial privatisation has little impact. This perspective ignores the role that the stock market can play in monitoring and rewarding managerial performance even when the government remains the controlling owner. Using data on Indian SOEs, Gupta (2006) found that partial privatisation has a positive impact on profitability, productivity, and investment.[16] However, an earlier study Naib (2003) found that in case of partial divestiture, where divested equity is thinly spread, there has been no improvement in profitability and operational efficiency.[17]

Distributional impact of privatisation

State-owned firms are public assets which earn a return for their owners. If the assets to be privatised are valued in such a way that their price represents the discounted sum of the profits to be earned from them, then privatisation means that the state is replacing an income stream with its discounted capital value in its asset portfolio. At the same time, the private sector is purchasing an asset which generates its full value over time from its annual earnings. However valuation of assets remains a complex issue.

If state-owned assets are transferred at below their market and or embedded value to those who are already wealthy, it would lead to increasing inequality. The state may do so based on the belief that particular private individuals are most likely to be able to improve company performance. But if the government reward their political supporters by awarding public assets, rather than being used to improve efficiency, privatisation may be employed by the ruling group as a mechanism to redistribute wealth and resources.

Estrin and Pelletier (2018) also bring out how selling key assets such as banks or resource companies to foreign firms may restrict the range of domestic policy and hinder long-term development.[18]

In Indian context, all these factors are relevant when the federal government is undertaking privatisation of Air India, airports, oil companies (BPCL), banks, and monetisation of assets on long term lease.

India has to be cautious in selling assets to elites which may concentrate political power and economic wealth into fewer hands. India's growth has been more unequal than in most other parts of the world. According to the World Inequality Report 2018, income inequality in India has increased since deregulation started in the 1980s, with the top 10% of earners accounting for 55% of the national wealth in 2016.[19] Successful privatisation requires transparent procedures and selection of methods to check on corruption.

References

1. Vickers, J. and G. Yarrow (1988). *Privatization: An Economic Analysis.* Cambridge, MA: MIT Press.

2. Megginson, W., and J. Netter (2001). 'From state to market: a survey of empirical studies on privatization.' *Journal of Economic Literature 39*(2): 321–89.

3. Kikeri, S., and J. Nellis (2004). 'An assessment of privatization'. *World Bank Research Observer 19*(1): 87–118.

4. Ehrlich, I., G. Gallais-Hamonno, Z. Liu, and R. Lutter (1994). 'Productivity growth and firm ownership: An empirical investigation'. *Journal of Political Economy 102* (5): 1006–38.

5. Majumdar, S. K (1996) . 'Assessing comparative efficiency of the state-owned, mixed, and private sectors in Indian industry'. *Public Choice 96*(1/2): 1–24.

6. Tian, G. (2000). 'State shareholding and corporate performance: A study of a unique Chinese data set'. Working Paper, London: London Business School.

7. Naib, S. (2004). 'Ownership, competition and efficiency: New evidence in Indian context', *Economic & Political Weekly* XXXIX(20): 2029–2035, 15 May.

8. Galal, A., L. Jones, P. Tandon, and I. Vogelsang (1994). *Welfare Consequences of Selling Public Enterprises*. Oxford: Oxford University Press.

9. Boardman, A., and A. Vining (1989). 'Ownership and performance in competitive environments: A comparison of the performance of private, mixed, and state-owned enterprises'. *Journal of Law Economics 32*(1): 1–33.

10. Frydman, R., C. Gray, M. Hessel, and A. Rapaczynski (1999). 'When does privatization work? The impact of private ownership on corporate performance in transition economies'. *Quarterly Journal of Economics 114*(4): 1153–91.

11. Dinc, S., and N. Gupta (2011). 'The decision to privatise: Finance and politics'. *The Journal of Finance* LXVI (1): 241–69.

12. Government of India, Ministry of Finance, *Economic Survey 2019–20*. www.indiabudget.gov.in/budget2020-21/economicsurvey/index.php

13. Megginson, W., R. Nash, and M. van Randenborgh (1994). 'The financial and operating performance of newly privatised firms: An international empirical analysis'. *Journal of Finance 49*(2): 403–52.

14. Megginson, W., and J. Netter (2001). 'From state to market: A survey of empirical studies on privatization.' *Journal of Economic Literature 39*(2): 321–89.

15. Li, B., W. L. Megginson, Z. Shen, and Q. Sun (2016). 'Do share issue privatizations really improve firm performance in China?' Working Paper, University of Oklahoma, www.efmaefm.org/0EFMAMEETINGS/EFMA%20ANNUAL%20MEETINGS/2016-Switzerland/papers/EFMA2016_0286_fullpaper.pdf

16. Gupta, Nandini (2005). 'Partial privatization and firm performance'. *The Journal of Finance*, LX(2): 987–1015.

17. Naib, Sudhir (2003). 'Partial divestiture and performance of Indian public sector enterprises'. *Economic and Political Weekly* XXXVIII(29): 3088–93.

18. Estrin, S. and A. Pelletier (2018) 'Privatization in developing countries: What are the lessons of recent experience?' *The World Bank Research Observer* 33(1), February 65–102, https://doi.org/10.1093/wbro/lkx007, can be accessed on https://academic.oup.com/wbro/article/33/1/65/4951686

19. IANS (2017). 'Top 10% earners have 55% of India's wealth: Report', *Financial Express*, 20 December. www.financialexpress.com/economy/top-10-earners-have-55-of-indias-wealth-report/982995/

3 The public sector in India

Public sector enterprises in India

For planning purpose, the public sector in India includes all activities funded out of the government's budget. Public sector covers government administration, departmental enterprises, and non-departmental enterprises.

The activities covered under the administrative departments relate to services like collection of taxes, general administrative services like police, external affairs, defence, community services such as education, health services; and economic services – agriculture, industry, transport, and construction.

The departmental enterprises are unincorporated enterprises owned and controlled by public authorities. The enterprises charge for the goods and services they provide like railways, ordnance factories, post and telegraph, irrigation, road and water transport, forests, mints, and state electricity boards.

The non-departmental financial and non-financial enterprises include government companies. According to the Companies Act 2013, a government company means any company in which not less than 51% of the paid up share capital is held by the Central/State government and includes a company which is a subsidiary company of such a government company (Section 2(45)). Government companies can be statutory corporations set up under the separate enactment of the legislature, or created by executive decision of government without the specific approval of parliament. Examples of statutory corporations include Air India, Oil and Natural Gas Corporation, Life Insurance Corporation, nationalised banks, state electricity boards, state transport corporations which have been constituted under a specific Act of Parliament. Most public sector companies in India are government companies. In this book and chapter we focus on Central Public Sector Enterprises.

DOI: 10.4324/9781003262213-4

India's industrial policy

Post independence in 1947, speedy economic development with social justice became the overriding goal for the Indian government. The State was perceived to be the driving force for this purpose. Jawaharlal Nehru, the first prime minister of post-independent India, envisaged the role of government-owned firms to scale the 'commanding heights of the economy'. According to Minhas (1974) apart from ideological preferences for the public sector, the planners believed that:[1]

- private investors may demand a higher risk premium for investment in some industries than would be socially justified;
- the scale of investment effort in heavy industries may be beyond the capital raising capacity of the private sector;
- the public sector, through appropriate price policy for its output, will generate profits for further investment in the economy;
- by production and or distribution of crucial inputs, the State will be able to control the private sector, and
- the employment and wage policy of the public sector can be directed to benefit disadvantaged groups in the society.

Industrial Policy Resolution of 1956

The Industrial Policy Resolution of 1956 stated that 'the adoption of the socialist pattern of society as the national objective, as well as the need for planned and rapid development, require that all industries of basic and strategic importance, or in the nature of public utility services should be in the public sector. Other industries, which are essential and require investment on a scale that only the State in the present circumstances could provide, have also to be in the public sector.' The Policy Resolution of 1956 classified industries into three categories:

SCHEDULE A: These comprised 17 industries such as arms, atomic energy, iron and steel, coal, mineral oils, mining, air and railway transport, generation and distribution of electricity and others.

These industries were to be the exclusive responsibility of the State.

SCHEDULE B: These comprised 12 industries such as a few mining industries, chemical industries, antibiotics, fertilisers, synthetic rubber, road transport, sea transport and others.

In these industries, the State would generally set up new enterprises while the private sector would be expected only to supplement the efforts of the State

SCHEDULE C: This category comprised all the remaining industries.

Industrial Policy Resolutions of 1977 and 1980 reiterated successive Government's faith in the public sector for rapid and sustained industrial development of the country.

Statement on Industrial Policy, 1991

The month of July in 1991 marked a turning point in contemporary Indian economic history. A new Congress led coalition government, under Prime Minister Narasimha Rao with Dr Manmohan Singh as Finance Minister had to deal with an exceptionally severe balance of payments crisis. In the previous 18 months, the country had gone through two unstable minority governments: Vishwanath Pratap Singh – December 1989 to November 1990, and Chandra Shekhar – November 1990 to June 1991.

Foreign exchange reserves had run down to $1.1 billion by the end of June 1991, barely enough for two weeks of imports, and there were widespread fears that India might be forced to default on its external debt payments.

The new government moved to contain the crisis through a stabilisation programme consisting of a reduction in the fiscal deficit, and currency devaluation. It also initiated a programme of structural reforms. The structural reforms were a distinct departure from the incremental changes attempted earlier. They signalled a clear shift towards a much more market oriented economy, with a much larger role for the private sector and greater openness to trade and foreign investment.

Ahluwalia (2019) summarised the major changes brought in by the Statement on Industrial Policy, 1991:[2]

1. Industrial licensing, which was earlier applicable for all industries except a defined list, was now abolished for all but a handful of industries. This meant investment in new plants and capacity expansion in existing plants could now be undertaken for a very wide range of industries without any approval from the central government. Since the location of industries was previously specified in the licence, the abolition of industrial licences also meant that

location was left to investors to decide, setting the stage for different states to compete with each other to attract private investment.

2. The list of 18 industries earlier reserved exclusively for the public sector was reduced to eight, and later this was further pruned.

   It may be noted that in March 2016, the Minister of State for Heavy Industries and Public Enterprises informed Rajya Sabha that only two industries are reserved for the public sector.[3] First, Atomic Energy (Production, Separation or enrichment of special fissionable materials and substances and operation of the facilities).[4] Second, railway operations other than construction, operation, and maintenance of (i) suburban corridor projects through PPP, (ii) high speed train project, (iii) dedicated freight lines, (iv) rolling stock including train sets, and locomotives/coaches manufacturing and maintenance facilities, (v) railway electrification, (vi) signalling systems, (vii) freight terminals, (viii) passenger terminals, (ix) infrastructure in industrial park pertaining to railway line/sidings including electrified railway lines and connectivity to main railway lines and (x) mass rapid transport systems.[5]

3. Earlier, the Monopolies and Restrictive Trade Practices (MRTP) Act provided that all investments by companies with total assets exceeding ₹ 1 billion needed special scrutiny to ensure that it would not increase concentration of economic power. These restrictions were abolished and the MRTP Act was to be used to check anticompetitive behaviour.

4. Foreign Direct Investment (FDI) was earlier allowed only in a defined list of high priority industries and each application needed to be cleared on a case-by-case basis, with foreign equity limited to 40%. FDI was now freely allowed up to 51% in this list and higher limits were considered on the merits of each case.

5. Foreign technology agreements, which earlier needed individual approval, became eligible for automatic approval provided royalties and technology fees were within specified parameters.

6. There was a very substantial liberalisation in trade policy. Capital goods, raw materials, components and other intermediate goods needed for production were made freely importable against tradable import licences. However, consumer goods remained on the banned list and were finally liberalised only in 2002.

7. A Committee on Tax Reforms was appointed, under the chairmanship of Raja Chelliah, to make recommendations for the reform of both direct and indirect taxes. It recommended a switch towards a regime of low tax rates with a broader base, a reduction in the

number of indirect tax rates, and a gradual reduction in customs duties to expose Indian industry to competition from abroad. The reduction in import duties was made possible by the devaluation in 1991 and the subsequent shift to a flexible exchange rate.

8. Financial sector reforms were seen as an essential accompaniment to industrial liberalisation, and a Committee on the Financial System under M. Narasimham recommended liberalisation of controls over the interest rates charged by banks for different types of loans, and introduction of tighter prudential and supervisory norms in line with the Basel I requirements that prevailed at the time. It also recommended abolishing government controls on capital issues in the stock market and on pricing of these issues, leaving both to be regulated by a statutorily empowered Securities and Exchanges Board of India (SEBI).

9. Qualified foreign institutional investors (FIIs) were allowed in 1992 to bring in capital to purchase shares in listed companies through the stock exchange. However there was a cap of 24% on the total equity in an individual company that could be held by FIIs.

10. As privatisation was simply not politically acceptable across the political spectrum, all that the government was willing to say was that 20% of the equity of profit making public sector enterprises (PSEs) would be disinvested to mutual funds and other financial institutions. It was also said that irreparable loss-making PSEs would be closed down, but this was never attempted.

Performance of Central Public Sector Enterprises (CPSEs)

The data on performance of Central Public Sector Enterprises is available in Government of India, Department of Public Enterprises, Public Enterprise Survey for the year 2018–19.[6] Public Enterprise Surveys for subsequent years were not published/uploaded on the Department of Public Enterprises website until July 2021.

Starting from five central government controlled enterprises in 1951 with a total investment of ₹29 crore (₹ 0.29 billion), there were 249 operating enterprises with the total investment of ₹ 1,640,628 crore (₹ 16,406.28 billion) on 31 March 2019. Production in sectors like coal, crude oil, and natural gas is predominately by CPSEs. In February 2018 the government approved opening of commercial coal mining for Indian and foreign companies in the private sector. Coal accounts for around 70% of the country's power generation. The private sector has contributed about 5% in total production per annum. Production

Table 3.1 Production of coal, crude oil, and natural gas

Production details

Details	2017–18	Share %	2018–19	Share%
Coal (in million tonnes)				
Coal India companies	567.37	84.01	606.89	83.11
Singarani Colleries Company Ltd (Andhra Government & Central Government Co.)	62.01	9.18	64.40	8.82
Captive production	37.07	5.49	49.88	6.83
Others	8.95	1.33	9.08	1.24
Total coal	675.40	100	730.25	100
Crude oil (in million metric tonnes)				
Central Public Sector Enterprises (CPSEs)	25.62	71.80	18.43 *	71.05
Private sector (incl. JVs)	10.06	28.20	7.51 *	28.95
Total	35.68	100	25.94 *	100
Natural gas (in billion cubic metres)				
Central Public Sector Enterprises (CPSEs)	26.28	80.58	27.19 *	83.05
Private sector (incl. JVs)	6.35	19.46	5.55 *	16.95
Total	32.63	100	32.74 *	100

Note. * up to December 2018.

Source: Public Enterprises Survey, 2018–19, Vol. I, p. 15.

details of coal, crude oil, and natural gas for Fiscal 2018 and 2019 are in Table 3.1.

In Fiscal 2019, out of 248 operating enterprises, 178 made profit and 70 made losses. An analysis of profit making enterprises reveal that the top 10 earned a net profit of ₹107,947 crore (₹ 1,079.47 billion) which is 61.83% of the profit of profit making enterprises. (Table 3.2). The top 10 loss making enterprises made a net loss of ₹ 29,751 crore (₹ 297.51 billion) which is 94.04% of the loss of loss making enterprises (Tables 3.3). On the whole for fiscal 2019, there was a net profit of ₹ 142,952 crore (₹ 1,429.52 billion) on a total investment of ₹1,640,628 crore (₹ 16,406.28 billion) which meant a return of 8.7%.

Other contributions of CPSEs

There are other contributions of CPSEs to the central exchequer by way of excise duty, customs duty, goods and services tax, corporate tax, interest on central government loans, dividend etc. increased to ₹ 368,803 crores (₹ 3,688.03 billion) in 2018–19, a 4.67% increase as

Table 3.2 Top 10 profit making CPSEs during 2018–19 (in crore of rupees)

S.No.	Name of CPSE	Net profit	Share (%)
1	ONGC	26,716	15.30
2	IOC	16,894	9.68
3	NTPC	11,750	6.53
4	Coal India	10,470	6.00
5	Power Grid	9,939	5.69
6	Bharat Petroleum Corporation Ltd	7,132	4.09
7	Power Finance Corporation Ltd	6953	3.98
8	Mahanandi Coalfields Ltd	6040	3.46
9	Hindustan Petroleum Corporation Ltd	6029	3.45
10	GAIL (India) Ltd	6026	3.45
	Top 10 profit making CPSEs (Total 1 to 10)	107,947	61.83
	Other CPSEs (168)	66,640	38.17
	Profit of profit making CPSEs (178)	174,587	100

Source: Government of India, Public Enterprises Survey, 2018–19, Volume 1, p. 4.

Table 3.3 Top 10 loss making CPSEs during 2018–19 (in crore of rupees)

S.No.	Name of CPSE	Net loss	Share (%)
1	BSNL	−14,904	47.11
2	Air India	−8475	26.79
3	MTNL	−3390	10.72
4	STC	−881	2.79
5	PEC	−500	1.58
6	Orissa Mineral Development Company Ltd	−452	1.43
7	MSTC Ltd	−324	1.03
8	National Textile Corporation Ltd	−315	0.99
9	Airline Allied Services Ltd	−297	0.94
10	Chennai Petroleum Corporation Ltd	−213	0.66
	Top 10 loss making CPSEs (Total 1 to 10)	−29,751	94.04
	Other CPSEs (60)	−1,884	5.96
	Loss of loss making CPSEs (70)	−31,635	100

Source: Government of India, Public Enterprises Survey, 2018–19, Volume 1, p. 5.

against the previous year of ₹ 352,361 crores (₹ 3,523.61 billion). The total market capitalisation of 56 CPSEs traded on stock exchanges of India was ₹ 1,371,116 crore (₹ 13,711.16 billion) as on 31 March 2019, a decrease of 9.82% from 31 March 2018. According to the Public Enterprises Survey, 2018–19 (Volume 1, p. 149) the number of employees in CPSEs as on 31 March 2019 was 15, 14,064 vis-à-vis 1,554,967 on 31 March 2018, a reduction of 40,903 employees including casual and contract.

In fiscal year 2021, the Union government collected ₹26,104 crore dividend from 23 PSUs that have announced their dividends. Bharat Petroleum Corp. Ltd (BPCL) leads the largest dividend-paying companies for FY 2021 with a dividend of ₹8,759.71 crore (₹ 87.60 billion) to the government. Analysis of the broader BSE 500 companies indicated that PSUs' share of profits rose from 18% in FY2018 to 28% in FY2021, but it has been consistently falling from 39% in FY2011.[7]

Shift in policy towards public sector enterprises

After announcing the Statement on Industrial Policy, 1991 the government appointed a Committee on Disinvestment under Dr C. Rangarajan, the then Governor of Reserve Bank of India. In its report given in 1993, it recommended holding of 51% or more equity by the government only in industries explicitly reserved for the public sector viz. coal and lignite; mineral oils; arms, ammunition, and defence equipment; atomic energy; radio-active minerals; and railway transport. In exceptional cases, such as the enterprises which had a dominant market share or where separate identity had to be maintained for strategic reasons, the committee recommended that public ownership can be kept at 26%, that is, disinvestment could take place to the extent of 74%. In all other cases, the committee recommended 100% disinvestment of government stake. However, no action was taken on the report as there was no political consensus about disinvestment to such an extent. During this phase, partial divestiture was undertaken in piecemeal manner with the sole aim to raise revenue.

The BJP-led National Democratic Alliance (NDA) coalition government under Atal Bihari Vajpayee took office in March 1998. It announced in the 1998–99 budget that government share holding in the SOEs will be brought down to 26% in the generality of cases. Further in March 1999, the government classified SOEs into strategic and non-strategic areas for the purpose of disinvestment. It was decided that the strategic SOEs would be those in the areas of arms and ammunition and the allied items of defence equipment, defence aircrafts and warships; atomic energy; and railway transport. All other SOEs were to be considered as non-strategic. Later, the government announced in the budget of 2000–2001 that it was prepared to reduce its stake in the non-strategic SOEs even below 26% if necessary. It further stated there would be closure of SOEs which cannot be revived.

Modern Foods India Ltd was the first such case of strategic disinvestment in January 2000 wherein 74% of the government equity was disinvested to a strategic partner with management control. Thereafter, major disinvestments were of BALCO in March 2001, CMC, HTL, IBP, VSNL, Paradeep Phosphates Ltd, Hindustan Zinc in 2001–2002, and Maruti Udyog and IPCL in May 2002. In addition to these SOEs, a number of ITDC hotels were sold outright. Arun Shourie, the Minister responsible for Disinvestment at the time, played a catalytic role in this exercise.

In 2004, there was a change in the federal government. The Congress-led United Progressive Alliance (UPA) with Manmohan Singh as the Prime Minister was in office from 2004 to 2014. During this period, the privatisation of SOEs was halted, and only partial disinvestment was resorted to.

But then in the general elections of 2014 and 2019, BJP-led National Democratic Alliance (NDA) formed the federal government with Narendra Modi as the Prime Minister of India. The policy shifted from partial disinvestment to strategic disinvestment. The Cabinet approved the new public sector enterprises policy and the same was announced by the Finance Minister in her budget speech on 1 February 2021.

Mandatory for CPSEs to plan asset sale, and dividend from year 2020

The government made it mandatory for Central Public Sector Enterprises (CPSEs) to outline a plan for non-core asset monetisation, payment of assured sum as dividend to the government, and take steps to increase market capitalisation of listed public sector undertakings. M-cap performance and asset monetisation were added to the set of parameters governing performance-related pay in memorandum of understandings (MOUs) being signed by the government and individual CPSEs starting 2021–22.[8]

New public sector enterprises policy for Atmanirbhar Bharat: 2021

The government revealed the broad contours of the policy in May 2020 as part of the Atmanirbhar Bharat package in the initial stages of the Covid-19 pandemic. The Prime Minister in a national address on 12 May 2020 announced the special economic and comprehensive package of ₹ 20 lakh crores – equivalent to 10% of India's GDP – to fight Covid-19 pandemic in India. He gave a clarion call for Aatma Nirbhar Bharat or Self-Reliant India Movement. He also outlined five pillars of Aatma Nirbhar Bharat – Economy, Infrastructure, System, Vibrant Demography, and Demand. Following the call of the Prime

Minister, the Finance Minister laid down the details of the Aatma Nirbhar Bharat Package in a string of press conferences. On 17 May 2020, FM informed that the government would announce new public sector policy for 'self-reliant' India, where all sectors are open to the private sector, while public sector enterprises would play an important role in defined areas.

The Cabinet Committee on Economic Affairs chaired by the Prime Minister approved the New Public Sector Enterprises Policy for Atmanirbhar Bharat on 27 January 2021. The same was announced by the Finance Minister Nirmala Sitharaman, in the budget speech on 1 February 2021.[9]

The key features of the policy were that the commercial public sector enterprises are classified into strategic and non-strategic sectors. The strategic sectors are:

  i) atomic energy, space and defence
 ii) transport and telecommunications
iii) power, petroleum, coal and other minerals
 iv) banking, insurance and financial services

In strategic sectors, there would be bare minimum presence of the public sector enterprises. The remaining CPSEs in the strategic sector would be privatised or merged or subsidiarised with other CPSEs or closed. In non-strategic sectors, CPSEs would be privatised, otherwise they would be closed.

However, the PSUs in the nature of development and regulatory authorities, autonomous organisations, trusts, development financing/refinancing institutions, some of which have been created through the Acts of Parliament, would be outside the purview of the new policy. According to DIPAM, such entities include major port trusts, Airports Authority of India (AAI), not-for-profit companies, PSUs that provide support to vulnerable groups, assist farmers, undertake security printing and minting, maintain critical data having bearing on national security and departments of the government, like railways and post, which undertake commercial operations with a development mandate.[10]

So only a handful of enterprises would remain in public sector. This was a complete break from the past and was beyond the Vajpayee-era privatisation drive, which was limited to a 'case-by-case' sale of entities in non-strategic sectors.

As mentioned earlier, it is interesting that the Rangarajan Committee report in 1993, had recommended holding of 51% or more equity by the government only in industries explicitly reserved for the public sector. In exceptional cases, such as the enterprises which had a dominant market share or where separate identity had to be maintained for strategic reasons, the committee recommended that public ownership can be kept at 26%. In all other cases, the committee recommended 100% disinvestment of government stake.

In a way, the present New Public Sector Enterprise Policy for Atmanirbhar Bharat (Self-reliant India) is quite in tune with what was recommended by Rangarajan Committee some 30 years back.

Another important aspect of the policy was monetisation of land assets. The Finance Minister stated that the non-core assets largely consist of surplus land with government Ministries/Departments and Public Sector Enterprises. Monetising of land can either be by way of direct sale or concession or by similar means. The FM proposed to use a *Special Purpose Vehicle* in the form of a company that would carry out this activity. Further, the FM announced that government would introduce a revised mechanism that would ensure timely closure of sick or loss making CPSEs.

The FM in the budget speech announced that two public sector banks and an insurance company will also be privatised. Being under intense pressure to raise resources, the union government has finally bitten the bullet. A disinvestment target of ₹₹1.75 lakh crore was estimated for FY21–22.

The Indian National Congress, president, Sonia Gandhi wrote in *The Hindu* on 4 March 2021 that the distress sale of national assets is unwise and the government's intent to offload public sector units and banks will only result in the long-term loss of public wealth. She wrote:

> executed carefully and strategically, disinvestment (which is the sale of a part of the government's shares in PSUs) can generate resources for the government, set the right incentives for their managements, and reward the investing public. In that spirit, Congress party 2019 Manifesto, promised a middle path to disinvest from only non-core, non-strategic public sector enterprises. But the Modi government has explicitly embraced 'privatisation' instead of 'disinvestment.' Its choice of language signals its intent. She alleged that in the garb of privatisation, valuable assets and profit-making companies will be undervalued and sold to cronies who will make a killing.[11]

The FM announced the National Monetisation Pipeline on 23 August 2021. The government planned to collect about ₹ 6 trillion over four years period ending 2024–25.The government stated that the assets are not being sold and would be handed back to government on completion of lease period.

References

1. Minhas, B. S. (1974). *Planning and the Poor*. New Delhi: S. Chand and Co.
2. JCER Working Paper, AEPR series No. 2018-1-2, Montek Singh Ahluwalia, 'India's economic reforms: Achievements and next steps' (Paper prepared for 27th AEPR conference, 7 April 2018, Tokyo). www.jcer.or.jp/jcer_download_log.php?f=eyJwb3N0X2lkIjoyOTIzMywiZmlsZV9wb3N0X2lkIjoiMjk0ODgifQ==&post_id=29233&file_post_id=29488
3. Ministry of Heavy Industries & Public Enterprises, *Revision of Policy towards Heavy Industries*, 3 March 2016.
4. Notification No. S.O. 2630(E) dated 19.10.2009 of Dept. of Industrial Policy & Promotion, Ministry of Commerce & Industry, Govt. of India.
5. Notification No. S.O. 2113 dated 22-8-2014 of Dept. of Industrial Policy & Promotion, Ministry of Commerce & Industry, Govt. of India.
6. Government of India, Public Enterprises Survey, 2018–19, Volume 1, https://dpe.gov.in/public-enterprises-survey-2018-19
7. Aswin Ramarathina, 'Govt eyes dividend windfall from PSUs ', *Hindustan Times*, 17 June 2021, p. 15, www.hindustantimes.com/business/government-eyes-dividend-windfall-from-psus-101623893359567.html
8. Nikunj Ohri, 'Planning for non-core asset sale, govt dividend now mandatory for PSUs', *Business Standard*, 12 December 2020, p. 5. www.business-standard.com/article/economy-policy/planning-for-non-core-asset-sale-govt-dividend-now-mandatory-for-psus-120121101464_1.html
9. Government of India, Budget 2021–2022, Speech of NirmalaI Sitharaman, Minister of Finance, 1 February 2021, www.indiabudget.gov.in/doc/budget_speech.pdf
10. Government of India, Ministry of Finance,Department of Investment and Public Asset Management, 'New Public Sector Enterprises (PSE) Policy for Atmanirbhar Bharat-regarding', Office Memorandum, 4 February 2021.
11. Sonia Gandhi, 'The distress sale of national assets is unwise', *The Hindu*, 4 March2021,www.thehindu.com/opinion/lead/the-distress-sale-of-national-assets-is-unwise/article33983312.ece

4   The global experience with privatisation

Privatisation in the 1980s

For decades prior to the 1980s, governments around the world increased the scope and magnitude of their activities, taking on a variety of tasks that the private sector previously had performed.

Federal Republic of Germany (FRG) in 1961 launched the first large-scale ideologically-motivated 'denationalisation' programme with the first majority sale in Volkswagen through a public share issue heavily tilted towards small investors and four years later it orchestrated a similar, but even larger, secondary share issue for VEBA. These two issues increased the number of shareholders in Germany from approximately 500,000 to almost three million.

Privatisation really came on the world stage in 1980s in United Kingdom. Margaret Thatcher's Conservative government came to power in May 1979. She was the Prime Minister till November 1990. The proceeds from the sale of state assets were below £500 million per annum in her first term of office, but after her re-election in June 1983, the privatisation programme accelerated dramatically. By the time of the 1987 election, the annual proceeds from asset sales were approaching £5 billion (Vickers and Yarrow, 1988).[1]

The major privatisations which took place in UK were British Petroleum (1979), British Aerospace (1981), Britoil (1982), National Freight Corporation (1982), Cable & Wireless (1983), Jaguar (1984), British Telecom (1984), British Aerospace (1985, final portion of holdings), British Gas (1986), British Airways (1987), Rolls Royce (1987), British Airports Authority (1987), British Steel (1988), and Royal Mail (2013).[2]

Margaret Thatcher (1993) wrote in her memoir, *The Downing Street Years*, that ownership by the state was just like ownership by an impersonal legal entity, it amounts to control by politicians and civil servants.

DOI: 10.4324/9781003262213-5

Whatever arguments there may-and should-be about means of sale, the competitive structures or the regulatory frameworks adopted in different cases, the fundamental purpose of privatisation must not be overlooked … For it meant that in some cases if it was a choice between having the ideal circumstances for privatisation, which might take years to achieve, and going for a sale within particular politically determined timescale, the second was the preferable option. Thatcher believed that the state should not be in business. The evidence of the lamentable performance of government in running any business – or indeed administering any service – according to her was so overwhelming that the onus should always be on statists to demonstrate why government should perform a particular function rather than why the private sector should not.[3]

The British privatisation programme favoured privatisation by wide public share holding. It brought out some features which are common to most public share offering privatisations. Not following these can put brakes on the programme, as India learned it a hard way when in September 2003, India's Supreme Court put on halt two oil public sector enterprises privatisation for want of Parliamentary approval.

The common features of privatisation programme in UK were:[4]

(i) Making business attractive to investors. In order to achieve a successful flotation, the nationalised enterprise must be attractive to investors. Often this meant that enterprises were restructured, certain parts were disposed of before the main sale, or the debt and tax liabilities were re-structured. This process sometimes resulted in the nationalised enterprise becoming profitable in the period immediately prior to privatisation, as it was in the case of British Steel.

(ii) Bringing legislative changes to change ownership. Formally nationalised industries often required legislative approval before they could be privatised because they were nationalised by Act of Parliament. For example, the Postal Services Act 2011 prepared Royal Mail for privatisation.

(iii) Meeting Stock Exchange requirements. In order to comply with Stock Exchange rules and to provide potential investors with all the information they need on the company, a 'prospectus' was always produced prior to privatisation.

(iv) Setting the share price. Setting the price of the shares was a crucial and sensitive part of the process. The most straightforward approach was a fixed-price offer, as happened with British Gas, in which a price for all the shares was set by the government. Another approach was a tender offer with a 'striking price', the price being determined by what investors are prepared to pay, up to a given amount. Often, share sales were over-subscribed, but when they were not, underwriters were often required to buy any remaining shares, as happened in the sale of the final tranche of BP shares in 1987.

(v) Marketing the offer: Ensuring that there is sufficient awareness and interest in the sale is an important part of the privatisation process. Often extensive marketing campaigns were used to sell shares to the public, the most famous of which was the 'Tell Sid' campaign used to market the sale of British Gas.

Now, we take the case of big ticket privatisation, British Telecom in November 1984, by far the largest equity offering in history to that time.

Case of privatisation of British Telecom

The British Telecommunication Act 1981 divided the Post Office Corporation into British Telecommunications (BT) and the Post Office. The Telecommunications Act made provision for BT to be privatised, for its monopoly over telephone services to be removed and for the setting up of the industry regulator – the Office of Telecommunications (Oftel). BT was privatised in three tranches in November 1984, December 1991, and July 1993. The November 1984 colossal share issue, by far the largest equity offering in history to that time, was met with strong demand by investors (including employees) both at home and abroad. It was a fixed price offer of 50% of the company at 130p a share. 3,012 million shares were floated on 16 November 1984. Up to 10% of the shares were reserved for eligible employees. Shareholders paid in three instalments. Subsequently, 26% of the company was subject to a combined public offer and International Tender offer of 1,600 million shares. Later the remaining 22% of shares were offered for sale. The gross proceeds in the three tranches were £3,916 million, £5,430 million, and £4,976 million. The BT sale proved that a global market for privatisation share issues existed and the size was not an impediment to privatisation.[5]

Sudhir Naib (2004) stated that after privatisation of British Telecom in UK, many other countries adopted privatisation. The next major country to adopt large-scale privatisation was France. The conservative Chirac government sold 22 major companies worth $12 billion in a 15 months period beginning in September 1986. The other countries were – Austria, Belgium, Holland, Jamaica, Japan, Spain, Sweden, and United States, adopted privatisation programmes. The major privatisations included BNP (France), Nippon Telephone and Telegraph (Japan), and Conrail (US). The privatisation programmes also spread to the developing countries in Latin America, East and South Asia, and Africa. While most of these programmes relied primarily on private sales (selling an SOE directly to another corporation), there were significant share issues also in Bangladesh, Brazil, Chile, Gambia, Malaysia, Mexico, Nigeria, Sierra Leone, Singapore, and Venezuela.[6]

The Mexican President Carlos Salinas announced in September 1989, plans to privatise the phone system and sell the state's 51% stake in Telmex. The government chose Goldman Sachs as advisor in this transaction for its experience in the privatisations of British Gas (1986), British Petroleum (1987), and Telefonica of Spain (1987). Privatisation of Mexico's telephone utility, Telefonos de Mexico (through a combined private sale and public share issue) made Mexico a magnet for foreign investments and greatly promoted its subsequent liberalisation.

By the end of the 1980s, sales of state enterprises worldwide had reached a total of over $185 billion.[7]

Privatisation in the 1990s

As the decade of the 1990s began, the privatisation shifted to Eastern Europe and the former Soviet Union. In Russia and elsewhere, proponents of rapid, mass privatisation of state-owned firms hoped that the profit incentives unleashed by privatisation would soon revive faltering, centrally planned economies. Writing in *The New York Times*, Jeffrey D. Sachs, the noted economist, stated that 'when the economic reforms got under way in 1992, Russia's vast natural resources provided unparalleled opportunities for theft by officials. Oil, gas, and metal ore deposits were nominally owned by the state and thus by nobody. They were ripe for stealing. Much of the income flowed to a few private pockets. Because of low interest rates and high inflation, many of the rubles loaned by banks were converted into dollars in the black market and stashed abroad'.[8]

Black, Kraakman, and Tarassova (2000) stated that Russia accelerated the self-dealing process by selling control of its largest enterprises cheaply to crooks, who transferred their skimming talents to the enterprises they acquired, and used their wealth to further corrupt the government. Lessons from privatisation in Russia were mass privatisation is likely to lead to massive self-dealing by managers and controlling shareholders unless a country has a good institutional infrastructure for controlling self-dealing.[9]

The mid 1990s also witnessed an acceleration of privatisation programmes in other parts of Europe. In terms of both scale and scope in the early 1990s, the Italian SOEs ranked high among OECD countries.

The three main conglomerates (IRI, ENI, and EFIM) employed over half a million people altogether in 1992. On the whole, the Italian SOEs was characterised by a disappointing performance and widespread inefficiency since 1970s. In the midst of political, economic, and financial crisis Italy launched a large scale privatisation programme in 1992. Here we take the case of privatisation of ENI. It is Italy's biggest listed company and a strategic investment for the state because of its key long-term gas contracts and rich dividend flows.

Case of privatisation of ENI

The credit for privatisation and transformation of ENI during 1992 to 1998 to a large extent goes to Franco Bernabe, the CEO. The company was plagued by a widely diversified portfolio ranging from oil to newspapers, and it was also drowning in debt. Overall, the company had 335 operating companies, and almost all of them were loosing money. In an interview with Professor Linda Hill and Suzy Wetlaufer, published in *Harvard Business Review*, July–August 1998 issue, he said, 'Believe me, when we started talking about privatisation; everyone said it could never be done. They said our legal problems and our logistical problems were insurmountable … In our case, the objective was very clear; we wanted the company privatised.'[10]

ENI divested its equity in tranches (1995, I tranche – 15%; 1996, II tranche – 15.82%; 1997, III tranche – 17.60%; 1998 IV tranche – 14.83%; 2001 V tranche – 5%). This resulted in privatisation of ENI to the extent of 68.25%.[11] Italy's Prime Minister Enrico Letta announced in November 2013, that the government would sell a 3% stake in ENI in 2014 as part of a wider privatisation programme to reduce public debt. He added that the state's stake would not fall below the key 30% level, due to a buyback programme already launched by ENI.[12] As of 4 February 2021, the state's total holding is 30.33%: Ministry of Economy and Finance – 4.37%, and state lender Cassa Depositi e Prestiti (CDP) 25.96%.[13]

Treuhandstalt (THA)

The 1990s also saw reactivation of privatisation in Germany following the collapse of communism in East Germany. Treuhandstalt (THA) was set up in March 1990 by the German Democratic Republic, and after reunification, the Treuhandstalt became a legally constituted entity under the legal and technical supervision of the Federal Ministry of Finance. Having completed the bulk of its task, the Treuhandstalt was wound up at the end of 1994. (For details, see Wendy Carlin and Colin Mayer (1994).)[14]

It has been estimated (Kikeri and Nellis, 2004, p. 89) that between 1990 and 1999, global proceeds totalled US$ 850 billion, growing from $30 billion in 1990 to $145 billion in 1999.[15]

The year-wise amount raised from privatisation from 1990 to 1999 is given in Table 4.1

Privatisation in the 2000s

Privatisation trends from 2000 to 2008

Post-2000, the transition states put much of their remaining portfolios on the market and did not use vouchers. These produced substantial revenues. Also, there was increasing importance of privatisation in East Asia, particularly China, where post-2000, numerous massive initial public offerings (IPOs) were launched. Privatisation proceeds in developing and emerging markets during 2000–08 are given in Table 4.2. The bulk of privatisation proceeds in South Asia's $ 17.45 billion, was realised in India (55%) followed by Pakistan (43%).

Privatisation trends since 2009

It has been noted (Estrin and Pelletier, 2018, pp. 68–9) that China has consistently been one of the top privatising country from 2009 to 2015. Aggregate privatisation deals in China totalled more than $40 billion in both 2013 and 2014. The five largest single deals outside the developed world in 2014 were realised in China, with the recapitalisation and primary share offering of CITIC Pacific Ltd, the private placement of BOE Technology Group, the primary-share IPO of Dalian Wanda Commercial, CGN Power, and HK Electrical Investments Ltd.

The authors estimated the global privatisation proceeds exceeding $1.1 trillion from January 2009 to November 2014, based on the data of Privatisation Barometer Report.[16]

Post-Covid privatisation and state ownership

Though the debate around the possibility of the coronavirus having leaked from the Wuhan lab in China was gaining pace across the world, the World Bank's East Asia and Pacific Economic Update, October 2020, forecasted that in stark contrast to the economies of its regional neighbors, China would grow by 2% in 2020.[17]

Table 4.1 Global proceeds from privatisation transactions, 1990–1999

	1990	1991	1992	1993	1994	1995	1996	1997	1998	1999
DEVELOPED COUNTRIES										
Australia	19	1,042	1,893	2,057	2,055	8,089	9,052	16,815	7,146	15,220
France				12,160	5,479	4,136	3,096	10,105	13,596	9,478
Italy			759	3,039	9,077	10,131	11,225	24,536	14,497	25,594
Japan					13,875		2,039		6,641	15,115
UK	12,906	21,825	604	8,523	1,341	6,691	6,695	4,544		
Others	7,635	1,371	4,058	8,772	15,314	3,440	32,236	30,700	47,976	32,403
DEVELOPED	20,506	24,238	7,314	34,551	47,141	48,327	64,343	86,700	89,856	97,810
DEVELOPING	12,658	24,242	26,180	23,663	21,717	21,903	25,400	66,573	49,308	44,076
GLOBAL TOTAL	33,218	48,480	33,494	58,214	68,858	70,230	89,743	1,53,273	1,39,164	1,41,886

Source: Based on World Bank (2001) and OECD (2001) data. Originally published in *Disinvestment in India: Policies, Procedures, Practice*, Copyright 2004 © Sudhir Naib. All rights reserved. Reproduced with the permission of the copyright holder and the publishers, SAGE Publications India Pvt Ltd, New Delhi (Table 4.1, p. 144).
(US dollars in millions)

Table 4.2 Privatisation proceeds in developing and emerging markets, 2000–2008 (US$ millions)

East Europe-Cental Asia	East Asia-Pacific	Sub-Saharan Africa	South Asia	Middle East, North-Africa	Latin America	Total
1,71,198	1,83,949	12,451	17,465	30,142	37,480	4,58,685

Source: Nellis, John, 'The international experience with privatization: Its rapid rise, partial fall and uncertain future', University of Calgary, The School of Public Policy, SPP Research Papers, Volume 5, Issue 3, January 2012: Table 3, p. 5. DOI: https://doi.org/10.11575/sppp.v5i0.42389, https://dev.journalhosting.ucalgary.ca/index.php/sppp/article/view/42389/30284

China's growth has been phenomenal. It has become the world's leading manufacturer, leading exporter, and by GDP measured at purchasing power parity, the world's largest economy. It has been noted (Megginson, 2017, p. 5) that China's GDP in 2000 at market prices was $1.21 trillion, and represented only about 3.6% of world GDP, it reached $11.06 trillion and 17.52% of world GDP by 2015. China's reliance on and support for state-owned and/or state-influenced 'national champions' in key industrial sectors was adopting the same model of 'state capitalism' that earlier Asian pioneers used successfully in their take-off phases.[18]

The Organisation for Economic Co-operation and Development (OECD), reported in June 2020 that governments are considering taking equity stakes or may be considering whether to do so in distressed firms among the crisis-response tools. The Covid-19 pandemic may result in increased state ownership or control of enterprises.[19] In contrast, Covid-19 has increased privatisation and asset monetisation in India to generate resources. The world has thus been witnessing two contradictory economic phenomena: continuing privatisation/ and monetisation of state assets by some government's like India, while some governments like OECD countries are considering taking equity stakes in distressed firms.

References

1. Vickers, J. and G. Yarrow (1988). *Privatization: An Economic Analysis*, Cambridge, MA: MIT Press.
2. Chris Rhodes, David Hough, and Louise Butcher, *Privatisation*, House of Commons, Library, Research Paper, 14/61, 20 November 2014: 15. https://researchbriefings.files.parliament.uk/documents/RP14-61/RP14-61.pdf

3. Margaret Thatcher (1993). *The Downing Street Years*. *HarperCollins Publishers*, London, 676–677.

4. Chris Rhodes, David Hough, and Louise Butcher, *Privatisation*, House of Commons, Library, Research Paper, 14/61, 20 November 2014: 5–6. https://researchbriefings.files.parliament.uk/documents/RP14-61/RP14-61.pdf

5. Chris Rhodes, David Hough, and Louise Butcher, *Privatisation*, House of Commons, Library, Research Paper, 14/61, 20 November 2014: 23. https://researchbriefings.files.parliament.uk/documents/RP14-61/RP14-61.pdf

6. Naib, Sudhir (2004). Originally published in *Disinvestment in India: Policies, Procedures, Practice, Copyright 2004 © Sudhir Naib*. All rights reserved. Reproduced with the permission of the copyright holder and the publishers, SAGE Publications India Pvt. Ltd, New Delhi, pp. 138–41.

7. Goodman, John B. and Loveman, Gary W. (1991). 'Does privatization serve the public interest?' *Harvard Business Review*, (November–December), https://hbr.org/1991/11/does-privatization-serve-the-public-interest

8. Jeffrey D. Sachs (1995), 'Why corruption rules Russia', *The New York Times*, 29 November 1995, Section A, p. 23, www.nytimes.com/1995/11/29/opinion/why-corruption-rules-russia.html

9. Black, B., Kraakman, R., and Tarassova, A. (2000). 'Russian privatization and corporate governance: What went wrong?' *Stanford Law Review 52*(6), 1731–1808. doi:10.2307/1229501, www.jstor.org/stable/1229501

10. Linda Hill and Suzy Wetlaufer (1998). 'Leadership when there is no one to ask: An interview with ENI's Franco Bernabe', *Harvard Business Review*, July–August. https://hbr.org/1998/07/leadership-when-there-is-no-one-to-ask-an-interview-with-enis-franco-bernab

11. Goldstein, Andrea (2003). 'Privatization in Italy 1993–2002: Goals, institutions, outcomes, and outstanding issues', CESifo Working Paper, No. 912, [Table 2 – Major privatisations in Italy since 1993]. Center for Economic Studies and ifo Institute (CESifo), Munich. www.cesifo.org/en/publikationen/2003/working-paper/privatization-italy-1993-2002-goals-institutions-outcomes-and

12. Giuseppe Fonte and Stephen Jewkes (2013). 'Italy's Eni stake sale implies 10 percent buyback program', *Reuters*, 21 November, www.reuters.com/article/us-eni-government/italys-eni-stake-sale-implies-10-percent-buyback-program-idUSBRE9AK10E20131121

13. ENI, www.eni.com/en-IT/about-us/governance/shareholders.html

14. Wendy Carlin and Colin Mayer (1994). 'The Treuhandanstalt: privatization by state and market'. In Olivier Blanchard, Kenneth Froot, and Jeffrey Sachs, eds, *Transition in Eastern Europe, Volume 2* (pp. 189–214). University of Chicago Press. https://core.ac.uk/download/pdf/6706321.pdf

15. Sunita Kikeri and Nellis, J. (2004). 'An assessment of privatization'. *The World Bank Research Observer 19*(1), 87–118.

16. Estrin, S. and A. Pelletier (2018), 'Privatization in developing countries: What are the lessons of recent experience?' *The World Bank Research Observer 33*(1), February, 65–102. https://doi.org/10.1093/wbro/lkx007

17. World Bank (2020). 'From containment to recovery: Economic update for East Asia and the Pacific', October. www.worldbank.org/en/region/eap/publication/east-asia-pacific-economic-update
18. Megginson, W. L. (2017), 'Privatization, state capitalism, and state ownership of business in the 21st century', *Foundations and Trends® in Finance* 11(1–2): 1–153. Accessed summary from www.nowpublishers.com/article/DownloadSummary/FIN-053.
19. OECD (2020). 'The Covid-19 crisis and state ownership in the economy: Issues and policy considerations', 25 June, www.oecd.org/coronavirus/policy-responses/the-covid-19-crisis-and-state-ownership-in-the-economy-issues-and-policy-considerations-ce417c46/

5 India's journey from partial divestiture to privatisation

1991–2021

Triggers for disinvestment

Fiscal distress

The Indian disinvestment programme was an offshoot of an unprecedented macroeconomic crisis during 1990–91. This was mainly due to the large imbalances on internal and external account. There was worsening of the fiscal deficit from 1985–86 onwards due to a steady increase in government expenditure, particularly non-plan expenditure. The fiscal deficit of the central government rose to 8.4% of GDP in 1990–91, an all time high. Further, the public debt to GDP ratio increased in 1980s and was 62.9% in 1990–91. This, coupled with the Gulf War in 1990–91 and the consequent rise of oil prices, further worsened the fiscal crisis. Erosion of confidence in the government's ability to manage the economy led to drying-up of the market for external commercial loans. The net outflow of non-resident Indian deposits also significantly added to the balance of payment crisis. Due to the deteriorating balance of payments situation, the Reserve Bank of India resorted to stringent contractionary measures through the monetary and credit policy instruments.

Notwithstanding these measures and the large drawings from the International Monetary Fund in July 1990 and January 1991, there was a sharp reduction in the foreign exchange reserves, only $1.1 billion enough for two weeks of imports during 1990–91. The immediate issue was India's struggle to avoid defaulting on loans. It had never defaulted since independence 44 years ago. India's foreign debt had climbed to about $72 billion, making it the world's third largest debtor after Brazil and Mexico, as against $20.5 billion in 1980.[1]

DOI: 10.4324/9781003262213-6

IMF conditionality – driver of Indian reforms?

It was in this situation of crisis that the Cabinet Secretary Naresh Chandra appraised the prime minister designate P. V. Narasimha Rao on 20 June 1991, a day before being sworn as PM, that under the looming political uncertainties, they had initiated preliminary negotiations with the International Monetary Fund (IMF) for a standby loan of $ 2.3 million for a 20 months period. After seeking some clarifications, the PM designate gave his go-ahead for further negotiations.[2] The IMF loan would hinge on a set of conditions demanding that India reduce its budget deficit, open its markets to foreign competition, diminish its maze of licensing requirements, cut subsidies, and liberalise investment.[3]

Structural conditionality, of which privatisation became an important component, was a common feature of both IMF and World Bank programmes as assumption of both institutions was that the private sector will be able to increase the efficiency of production. Conditionality was thus a tool to pressure borrowing countries to privatise inefficient state enterprises. However, the decision regarding what to divest and on what scale, remained the government call.

The newly elected Congress-led government with Rao as Prime Minister, and Manmohan Singh as Finance Minister launched a programme of economic reforms in July 1991. Earlier in the day, before the Union Budget was presented on 24 July 1991, the Statement on Industrial Policy was tabled in the Parliament. The government adopted a dual strategy – fiscal measures to bring about macroeconomic stabilisation and structural reforms in the industrial and trade policy. These reforms were distinct precisely because they recognised the need for a system change, involving liberalisation of government controls, a larger role for the private sector and greater integration with the world economy. As privatisation was not politically acceptable across the political spectrum, the government announced that 20% of the equity of profit making public sector enterprises (PSEs) would be disinvested to mutual funds and other financial institutions. It was also said that irreparable loss-making PSEs would be closed down, but this was not attempted (see Chapter 3 – 'The public sector in India', for summary of major changes brought in by the Statement on Industrial Policy, 1991).

There has been much speculation that whether the India's reform agenda was thrust upon the Indian government by the IMF as part of its assistance program. Montek Singh Ahluwalia, who was then the Deputy Chairman of the Planning Commission, wrote and spoke about the 1991 reforms on the CNBC TV 18 interview on 24 July 2021 that the ideas implemented in the reform had been extensively discussed domestically, well before the crisis, and while they figured in the conditionality associated with the Fund's assistance, the IMF was not the principal driver. It would be more accurate to say that reformers in the government saw the crisis as opportunity to implement changes that were being discussed earlier, but were politically not acceptable.[4]

Politics of privatisation

Divestiture is a politically risky proposition. It may be unpopular with the general public because of high short-term costs. The costs of privatisation, just like most structural economic reforms, occur before the benefits of the policy accrue. For example, privatisation may cause an increase in consumer prices in the short term as price controls and subsidies are removed whereas the efficiency gains of privatisation will take a longer period to percolate down. Similarly, employee retrenchment at SOEs, a cost of privatisation, may be required before the gains of the privatisation.

Dinç and Gupta (2011) based on a study of Indian SOEs conclude that while the benefits of privatisation, such as efficiency improvements, are dispersed across the population, the costs are likely to be geographically concentrated among a small group, such as the local employees of government firms. The public too may perceive privatisation negatively as an unequal transfer of public assets to private owners. This could result in a decrease in voter support for the governing party in the region where the firm is located. The effect of a backlash on electoral outcomes will be greater if the governing party faces a close race with other political parties in that region.[5]

Taking politically risky decision to privatise depends on the ideology of the ruling political party. Ideologically, left-leaning governments are associated with lower volumes of privatisation and go for partial divestiture; given the negative dislocating effect that privatisation will have on their core support. The right-leaning parties are associated with higher volumes of privatisation. Generally coalition governments where the ruling party is in minority do not take an unpopular decision to privatise.

Criteria for selection of SOEs for privatisation

Is there a criteria for selection of SOEs for privatisation? From theoretical perspective one may discuss criteria of comparative advantage, and net economic yield.

Comparative advantage

Ramanadham (1991) advocates that where a public enterprise loses its comparative advantage, it is preferable to privatise it. The comparative advantage is to be measured in terms of the commercial returns, social returns, and a desired trade-off between them. The social-financial return combinations would be dissimilar among different enterprises or sectors, and hence the concept of comparative advantage has to be addressed in an enterprise-specific and time-specific manner.[6]

Net economic yield

The criterion for divestiture is net economic yield generated by the enterprise as state owned entity and as privatised entity. Two distinct elements affect this difference: the transfer of funds from the private sector to the public sector in connection with purchase of enterprise and the transfer of productive facilities from the public sector to the private sector.

The value to society under public operation is the present value of expected net benefits accruing to society as a whole from the continued public operation of the enterprise. As the government is concerned about overall welfare of society, it must also consider the firm's performance after sale that is social value under private operation. It is the present value of expected net benefits accruing to society as a whole from the private operation of enterprise. Jones et al. (1990) suggested that an asset should be sold only if the seller is better off after the sale, i.e. the change in welfare is positive.[7]

Another aspect is how the sale proceeds are used. This depends on the difference between the private and government revenue multipliers.[i]

Whenever social welfare is higher under private ownership than public, and government revenue multiplier greater than private profit multiplier, the price is of no consequence, and the government should be willing to pay the private sector to take over the enterprise. This might happen, if the enterprise is loss making under government operation but becomes viable under private ownership without large deleterious welfare effects on consumers or workers.

Influence of political and financial factors

Dinc and Gupta (2011) using Indian data from the 1990–2004 periods, empirically found that profitable firms and firms with a lower wage bill are likely to be privatised early and that the government delays privatisation in regions where the governing party faces more competition from opposition parties.[8]

Evolving policy on disinvestment

The journey from disinvestment to privatisation can be broadly put in four phases – the first from 1991–92 to 1997–98 under Congress and later Congress supported United Front Government, the second from 1998–99 to 2003–04 under National Democratic Alliance (NDA) government led by Bharatiya Janta Party (BJP), the third from 2004–05 to 2013–14, under UPA government led by Congress party, and the fourth from 2014–15 onwards under NDA government led by BJP. Broadly the Congress led governments' resorted to partial disinvestment of PSEs while the BJP led governments pursued strategic disinvestment leading to management transfer to the private entity.

The first phase: 1991–92 to 1997–98

In the background of fiscal situation becoming grim in 1991, the government considered the possibility of raising resources through divestment. Department of Economic Affairs, Government of India, submitted a paper to this effect in February 1991 to the Cabinet Committee on Political Affairs (CCPA). The CCPA gave general approval to pursue the approach of divestment. Thereafter, the first public announcement of the Government decision to disinvest up to 20% of its equity in selected Public Sector Undertakings was made on 4 March 1991 at the time of presenting Union government's interim budget for 1991–92 by Chandrashekhar government. The newly elected coalition government of Congress under Prime Minister P. V. Narasimha Rao in July 1991 reiterated the earlier announcement about disinvestment of 20% equity in selected SOEs. During the first phase 1991–92 to 1997–98, partial divestiture was undertaken. The other development during this period was institutionalising the disinvestment process by constituting Disinvestment Commission.

Institutionalising the disinvestment process

In February 1992, the government constituted a committee to institutionalise the disinvestment process under V. Krishnamurthy, Member Planning Commision. In November 1992, the Committee was reconstituted under Dr C. Rangarajan, Governor Reserve Bank of India. The Committee made far reaching recommendations in its report given in April 1993. It recommended holding of 51% or more equity by the government, only in industries explicitly reserved for the public sector viz. coal and lignite; mineral oils; arms, ammunition, and defence equipment; atomic energy; radio-active minerals; and railway transport. In exceptional cases, such as the enterprises which had a dominant market share or where separate identity had to be maintained for strategic reasons, the committee recommended that public ownership can be kept at 26%, that is, disinvestment could take place to the extent of 74%. In all other cases, the committee recommended 100% disinvestment of government stake. However, no action was taken on the report as there was no political consensus about disinvestment to such an extent. During this phase, partial divestiture was undertaken in piecemeal manner with the sole aim to raise revenue. From June 1996, United Front, a coalition government of 13 political parties remained in power till March 1998.

Disinvestment Commission

The United Front government constituted Public Sector Disinvestment Commission in August 1996 for a period of three years under G. V. Ramakrishna, former Chairman, Securities and Exchange Board of India. The main objective was to prepare an overall long-term disinvestment programme for public sector undertakings referred to the Commission. This inter alia included determining the extent of disinvestment, and supervising the overall sale process. As the Disinvestment Commission was critical of the government about slow progress in implementation of its recommendations, the powers of the Commission were axed in January 1998, and its role was diluted by taking out the overall monitoring and supervisory functions from its ambit. In all, the government referred 72 enterprises to the Commission but later withdrew eight enterprises. Out of the remaining 64 enterprises, the Commission did not consider six as they were already under reference to Board for Industrial and Financial Reconstruction (BIFR). The Commission was thus left with 58 enterprises.

The Commission examined each PSE and classified it as strategic or non-strategic. According to the Commission, strategic units are those engaged in defence and security-related production. In such units, government holding could be maintained at 100%. The non-strategic PSEs were classified as either core or non-core. The classification of PSE in core or non-core has been made by taking into account the structure of the industry, the competitiveness of the market in which it operates, its market share, and the public purpose (if any) served by it.

The Commission opined that core group is that which is capital or technology intensive and there is a tendency towards an oligopolistic market structure. Examples of such cases according to the Commission were telecom, power generation and transmission, petroleum exploration, and refining industries. The Commission felt that in such areas presence of public sector will be necessary for sometime as a countervailing force and recommended disinvestment up to 49% in core area for the present.

According to the Commission, non-core PSEs were in those areas, where private investments have grown considerably and markets are fully contestable. For non-core PSEs, Commission was of the view that it would be desirable to disinvest up to 74% or more. Withdrawal from non-core sectors was indicated on considerations of a long-term efficient use of capital, growing financial inviability, and the compulsions for these PSEs to operate in an increasingly competitive environment.

With this framework in place, out of the total 58 PSEs examined by it, the Commission categorised 14 PSEs in core group and 44 in non-core group. Recommendations for all these enterprises were given in 12 reports by August 1999. In majority of cases, it recommended strategic sale with transfer of management control. The Commission lapsed on 30 November 1999.

Reconstituted Disinvestment Commission

The NDA government reconstituted the Disinvestment Commission in July 2001 after more than a year and a half of the lapse of the earlier Commission. The Commission was reconstituted under the chairmanship of Dr R. H. Patil for a period of two years. The Commission's role was that of an advisory body to advice on disinvestment in those enterprises that are referred to it. The Commission gave recommendations in 13 reports (Report XIII to Report XXV). In all, the two Disinvestment Commissions gave recommendations in respect of 92 Central Public Sector Enterprises in 25 reports. See Appendix 'B' for list of CPSEs considered by the Disinvestment Commissions.

Disinvestment receipts and methodology used

During 1991–92 to 1997–98, the federal government disinvestment receipts was ₹11,251 crore, and the methodology used for disinvestment was Public Offer of Shares, and Auction to Financial Institutions. Details can be seen in Appendix 'C'.

The second phase: 1998–99 to 2003–04

After the general elections in 1998, the Bharatiya Janta Party (BJP) led coalition National Democratic Alliance (NDA) government under the Prime Minister Atal Bihari Vajpayee took office in March 1998. The major shift in this phase was that the government moved from partial divestiture to strategic sale. It announced in the 1998–99 budget that government share holding in the SOEs will be brought down to 26% in the generality of cases. However, the dilution of government stake would not be automatic and the manner and pace of doing so would be worked out on a case-to-case basis.

In March 1999, the government classified SOEs into strategic and non-strategic areas for the purpose of disinvestment. It was decided that the strategic SOEs would be those in the areas of arms and ammunition and the allied items of defence equipment, defence aircrafts and warships; atomic energy; and railway transport. All other SOEs were to be considered as non-strategic.

The other major milestone in this phase was creation of Department of Disinvestment in December 1999 which was henceforth to act as a nodal agency for disinvestment. The Department of Disinvestment was upgraded to Ministry in September 2001.

The government announced in the budget of 2000–2001 that it was prepared to reduce its stake in the non-strategic SOEs even below 26% if necessary. It further stated closure of SOEs which cannot be revived.

Moving from partial disinvestment to privatisation

During this phase, the Vajpayee government moved from partial disinvestment to privatisation where assets were transferred to private hands. Modern Foods India Ltd (MFIL) was the first such case in January 2000, wherein 74% of the government equity was disinvested to Hindustan Lever Limited (HUL), a strategic partner with management control.

Major strategic disinvestments in 2001 and 2002 were that of Bharat Aluminum Company Ltd (BALCO) and Hindustan Zinc Ltd (HZL) to Sterlite Industries Ltd, CMC to Tata Consultancy Services, Hindustan Teleprinters Ltd (HTL) to Hindustan Futuristic Communications, Videsh Sanchar Nigam Ltd (VSNL) to Tata group, Paradeep Phosphates Ltd to Zuari Maroc Phosphates Pvt Ltd, Maruti Udyog to Suzuki, Indian Petrochemicals Corporation Ltd,(IPCL) to Reliance Petro Investments, IBP to Indian Oil Corporation (IOC) another CPSEs. In addition to these CPSEs, a number of ITDC hotels were sold outright from November 2001 to July 2002.

It is of interest to note that except Modern Foods India Ltd, all other cases took place under Arun Shourie, an eminent economist, journalist, and author who had earlier worked in the World Bank, and was the Minister for Disinvestment under Atal Bihari Vajpayee. However, it is unfortunate that even after nearly two decades, Shourie is still haunted by a case filed against him alleging irregularities in the sale of Udaipur's Laxmi Vilas Palace Hotel in 2002. Both the Central Bureau of Investigation (CBI) and a Division Bench of High Court had concluded that there was no procedural violations in the sale of the hotel. The case was once again opened in 2014 with an anonymous complaint. Shourie had to come to Jodhpur to appear before the court despite his poor health in 2020.[9]

We discuss below the case of Modern Foods, the first one to be disinvested / privatisatised.

Modern Foods India Ltd (MFIL)

MFIL was the first public sector which was disinvested/privatised in January 2000, wherein 74% of the government equity was disinvested to Hindustan Lever Limited (HUL), a strategic partner with management control. Modern Foods had over 40% of the bread market in India. HUL paid ₹ 10.5 million for 74% of the shares. Later the government sold the remaining 26% to HUL for ₹ 4.4 million in November 2002. HUL sold the company in April 2016 to Everstone Capital . In February 2021, Everstone Capital sold its Modern Foods to Mexico's largest food and bakery company Grupo Bimbo in a deal worth ₹700 crore (7 billion).[10]

Disinvestment proceeds from 1998–89 to 2003–04 and
methodologies used

The disinvestment proceeds from 1998–89 to 2003–04 was ₹29,990 crore and the methodologies used were Strategic sale to private entities, Public Offer of Shares, and Auction to Financial Institutions/Private entities, Sale to Employees. Also CPSE to CPSE sale was done. Details can be seen in Appendix 'C'.

The third phase: 2004–05 to 2013–14

In 2004, with the change in the Government, there was a change in the outlook of disinvestment policy. In May 2004, the Congress led UPA government under the Prime Minister Manmohan Singh adopted National Common Minimum Programme, which also included policy with respect to the Public Sector. The UPA Government pledged to devolve full managerial control and commercial autonomy to successful, profit-making companies operating in competitive environment; and they won't be privatised. 'Navratna' companies can raise resources from the capital market and efforts to be made to modernise and restructure sick PSEs. To signal the change in policy, the Ministry of Disinvestment was made a Department of Disinvestment under the Ministry of Finance in May 2004.

The Government favoured sale of small proportions of its equity through Initial Public Offer (IPO)/Follow on Public Offer (FPO) without changing the character of PSEs. It approved listing of unlisted profitable CPSEs subject to residual equity of the Government remaining at least 51% and Government retaining the control of management.

In November 2009, Government approved that the already listed profitable CPSEs (not meeting mandatory shareholding of 10%) are to be made compliant by 'Offer for Sale' by Government or by the CPSEs through issue of fresh shares or a combination of both. Unlisted CPSEs with no accumulated losses and having earned net profit in three preceding consecutive years are to be listed. In all cases of disinvestment, the Government would retain at least 51% equity and the management control.

Disinvestment proceeds from 2004–05 to 2013–14 and methodologies used

The disinvestment proceeds from 2004–05 to 2013–14 was ₹114,045 crore and the methodologies used were Public Offer of Shares, and Auction to Financial Institutions, Sale to Employees, and Institutional Placement and CPSE to CPSE sale. Details can be seen in Appendix 'C'.

The fourth phase: 2014–15 to 2020–21

Modi's first term as Prime Minister

In the general elections of 2014, BJP emerged as the single largest party and BJP-led National Democratic Alliance (NDA) formed the union government under Narendra Damodardas Modi, as Prime Minister in May 2014. In April 2016, the Department of Disinvestment was renamed as Department of Investment and Public Asset Management (DIPAM) under Ministry of Finance.[11]

One of Modi's slogan in elections was 'Minimum Government, Maximum Governance'. However, only minority stakes in several government corporations were sold to reduce the fiscal deficit. Often government corporations with high reserves were asked to buy out the government's stock in other corporations. This balance sheet jugglery changed nothing in reality, but it cut the fiscal deficit. Modi government attempted only one privatisation in 2018, that of Air India, but so many conditions were attached to it that there were no bidders.

For strategic disinvestments in CPSEs, CCEA mandated a panel, a so-called Alternative Mechanism (AM) headed by finance minister to oversee the asset sale process in 2017. In March 2019, the CCEA chaired by the Prime Minister approved delegation of the following to Alternative Mechanism in all the cases of Strategic Disinvestment of CPSEs where CCEA has given 'in principle' approval for strategic disinvestment:[12]

(i)   The quantum of shares to be transacted, mode of sale, and final pricing of the transaction or lay down the principles/ guidelines for such pricing; and the selection of strategic partner/ buyer; terms and conditions of sale; and

(ii) To decide on the proposals of CGD with regard the timing, price, the terms and conditions of sale, and any other related issue to the transaction.

Modi's second term as Prime Minister

In general elections held in April–May 2019, Bharatiya Janata Party (BJP) had a landslide victory and won 303 Lok Sabha seats, a significant improvement on its previous 282 tally in 2014. A party needs to win 272 seats for a majority in parliament. Emboldened by a decisive re-election that saw the BJP return with a full majority in Parliament, the government first went for fulfilling its political electoral promises which included abolishing Article 370, fast-tracking the construction of the Ram temple in Ayodhya, and passing the Citizenship Amendment Act (CAA). The Prime Minister Modi set an ambitious target of doubling the size of the Indian economy to USD 5 trillion by 2024 and opened up several sectors to foreign investment. He also announced important reform to provide piped drinking water to all rural households by 2024.

Slowdown of economy in 2019

After demonetisation in November 2016, there was slowdown of economy and rise in unemployment. While it seemed that things were looking better, the economy again slowed down in 2019. In December 2019, Harvard University published a paper authored by Arvind Subramanian, and Josh Felman that the growth has slowed down.[13] The year 2019 was not the year when the economy has been hit by any of the standard triggers of slowdowns, what Harish Damodaran had called the 3 Fs. Food harvests haven't failed. World fuel prices haven't risen. The fiscal has not spiraled out of control.[14]

The Reserve Bank of India, the central bank, in its Annual Report for the year 2019–20 stated that until the onset of Covid-19, the moderation in India's growth trajectory reflected both global and domestic (Para 1.9). The government and RBI tried vigorously to bring the economy back to health. The government introduced a large corporate tax cut in the hope of reviving investment; and the RBI carried out a series of policy rate reductions, a cumulative 135 basis points from February 2019 to February 2020 (Para 1.10).[15] The RBI further reduced the policy repo rate by 115 basis points during March 2020 to May 2020 to 4%. Taking into account the earlier cut of 135 bps during February 2019 to February 2020, the cumulative reduction in the policy rate was 250 bps (Para 1.22 of the RBI Annual Report 2020–21).[16] This reduction has been more than any other central bank in the world over the period and one of the largest rate reductions in India's history in the hopes of reviving lending.

Privatisation push

On 20 November 2019, the government announced that full management control will be ceded to buyers of Bharat Petroleum Corporation Ltd (BPCL), Shipping Corporation of India (SCI) and Container Corporation of India Ltd (CONCOR).[17] On 8 January 2020, strategic disinvestment was approved for Minerals & Metals Trading Corporation Limited (MMTC), National Mineral Development Corporation (NMDC), MECON, and Bharat Heavy Electricals Ltd (BHEL).[18]

Disinvestment proceeds from 2014–15 to 2020–21 and methodologies used

The disinvestment proceeds from 2014–15 to 2020–21 (seven years) was ₹360,531 crore (₹ 3.60 trillion) as per BSE PSU data (see Appendix 'C'). However, Department of Investment and Public Asset Management, (DIPAM), Ministry of Finance data records ₹ 362,756 crore (₹ 3.62 trillion) as worked out from Appendix 'A'.

The methodologies used were Public Offer of Shares, Sale to Employees, Buy Back, Block Deals, CPSE to CPSE sale, and Exchange Traded Funds. A consolidated list of methodologies used for disinvestment of CPSEs from 1991–92 to 2020–21 is given in Appendix 'C' along with what each of these methodologies mean. According to BSE PSU data the total amount raised from 1991–92 to 2020–21 was ₹ 515,786 crore.

Disinvestment policy, 2020

On 10 February 2020 the Government informed Lok Sabha, Parliament of India, that the current disinvestment policy of the Government comprises of strategic disinvestment and minority stake sale.

(a) Strategic disinvestment is by way of sale of substantial portion of Government shareholding in identified CPSEs up to 50% or more, along with transfer of management control.

(b) Minority stake sale in listed CPSEs was to meet minimum public shareholding norms of 25 % as per SEBI regulations. While pursuing this objective of disinvestment, the Government will normally retain majority shareholding, i.e. at least 51% and management control of the CPSE. In select CPSEs Government may reduce equity below 51%, while retaining management control on a case to case basis. However, no such CPSEs have been approved by Government so far, in which GoI equity can be reduced below 51%.

The government clarified that profitability/loss of CPSE is not the relevant criteria for disinvestment. The Government has 'in principle' approved strategic disinvestment in 34 CPSEs since 2016, which are profit-making or loss-making, or CPSEs which may have made profits in some financial years and losses in some other financial years.[19]

The list of privatised CPSEs with details of new owners is at Appendix 'D', and the list of CPSEs approved 'in-principle' by the Cabinet Committee on Economic Affairs (CCEA) for strategic disinvestment is at Appendix 'E'.

Covid-19 pandemic and new policy measures

A once-in-a-century pandemic devastated most of the world's economies in 2020 and took its heavy toll on India. The Prime Minister Modi imposed a nationwide lockdown on the evening of 24 March 2020. The lockdown measures imposed to contain the spread of Covid-19 affected employment, business, trade, manufacturing, and services activities. The country's GDP growth turned negative for the first time in 40 years and an estimated 122 million workers found themselves without jobs in the ensuing lockdown. According to a BBC News report on 6 May 2020, of these 122 million, 91.3 millions were small traders and labourers. Also, salaried workers (17.8 million) and self-employed people (18.2 million) have also lost work.[20]

The Prime Minister declared a Covid relief package of INR 20 trillion (₹20 lakh crore) about ~USD 260 billion on 15 May 2020. The details of the stimulus package were outlined by the Union Finance Minister Nirmala Sitharaman under Atmanirbhar Bharat on 17 May 2020.[21]

The New Public Sector Enterprises Policy for Atmanirbhar Bharat was announced by the Union Finance Minister Nirmala Sitharaman, in the budget speech on 1 February 2021.The key features of the policy were that the commercial public sector enterprises are classified into strategic and non strategic sectors. In strategic sectors, there would be bare minimum presence of the public sector enterprises. The remaining CPSEs in the strategic sector would be privatised or merged or subsidiarised with other CPSEs or closed. In non-strategic sectors, CPSEs will be privatised, otherwise shall be closed.[22]

Note

i To see the difference between the private and government revenue multiplier, one has to compare the value of a rupee of private consumption with a rupee of government revenue. If additional revenue of Rs.100 (from sale of enterprise) allows the government to reduce taxes on consumption by, say worth Rs.125 to society, then the government revenue multiplier is 1.25. Also, a rupee of profits can be worth more than a rupee of consumption, so that there is a private profit multiplier that is greater than unity. This is when profits create investment which in turn creates a stream of consumption whose present value is greater than a rupee. However, when an economy is highly distorted by taxes and capital market imperfections, each of these multipliers may instead be less than one, i.e. revenues or profits may be less valuable than consumption.

References

1. Bernard Weinraub (1991), 'Economic crisis forcing once self-reliant India to seek aid', *The New York Times*, 29 June 1991, www.nytimes.com/1991/06/29/world/economic-crisis-forcing-once-self-reliant-india-to-seek-aid.html

2. P. Raman, '30 years ago, 90 mins that changed India's history', *Indian Express*, 13 June 2021, https://indianexpress.com/article/opinion/columns/30-yrs-ago-90-mins-that-changed-indias-history-7356387/
3. Bernard Weinraub, 'Economic crisis forcing once self-reliant India to seek aid', *The New York Times*, 29 June 1991, www.nytimes.com/1991/06/29/world/economic-crisis-forcing-once-self-reliant-india-to-seek-aid.html
4. JCER Working Paper, AEPR series No. 2018-1-2, Montek Singh Ahluwalia, 'India's economic reforms: Achievements and next steps' (Paper prepared for 27th AEPR conference, 7 April 2018, Tokyo). www.jcer.or.jp/jcer_download_log.php?f=eyJwb3N0X2lkIjoyOTIzMywiZmlsZV9wb3N0N0X2lkIjoiMjk0ODgifQ==&post_id=29233&file_post_id=29488   and CNBC TV 18 Interview, www.cnbctv18.com/economy/montek-singh-ahluwalia-on-how-1991-reforms-were-announced-10096411.htm
5. Dinc, S., and N. Gupta (2011). 'The decision to privatise: Finance and politics'. *The Journal of Finance* LXVI(1): 241–69.
6. Ramanadham, V. V. (1991). 'Comparative advantages of enterprise models – a conceptual analysis'. In S. R. Mohnot (ed.), *Privatization-Options and Challenges*, Centre for Industrial and Economic Research, New Delhi.
7. Jones, L. P., P. Tandon, and I. Vogelsang (1990). *Selling Public Enterprises: A Cost Benefit Methodology*, Cambridge, MA, MIT Press.
8. Dinc, S., and N. Gupta (2011). 'The decision to privatise: Finance and politics'. *The Journal of Finance* LXVI(1): 241–69.
9. Deep Mukherjee, 'Explained: The CBI order against Arun Shourie', *The Indian Express*, 18 September 2020, https://indianexpress.com/article/explained/arun-shourie-cbi-court-criminal-case-rajasthan-laxmi-vilas-palace-hotel-6600843/
10. The Economic Times, 'Mexico's Grupo Bimbo buys iconic bread brand Modern Foods', 25 February 2021, p. 5.
11. Financial Express, 'Department of Disinvestment renamed Dipam', *Financial Express*, 20 April 2016, www.financialexpress.com/economy/department-of-disinvestment-renamed-as-dipam/240340/
12. PIB, Government of India, 'Cabinet approves procedure and mechanism for Strategic Disinvestment of the CPSEs – delegation thereof', 7 March 2019, https://pib.gov.in/PressReleseDetail.aspx?PRID=1567764
13. Arvind Subramanian and Josh Felman, Harvard Kennedy School, CID Faculty Working Paper No. 370, December 2019 'India's great slowdown: What happened? What's the way out?', www.hks.harvard.edu/sites/default/files/centers/cid/files/publications/faculty-working-papers/2019-12-cid-wp-369-indian-growth-diagnosis-remedies-final.pdf
14. Harish Damodaran, 'This is India's first ever slowdown at a time of political as well as macroeconomic stability', *The Indian Express*, 30 November 2019, https://indianexpress.com/article/opinion/columns/a-different-downturn-gdp-growth-economic-slowdown-6143309/

15. Reserve Bank of India, Annual Report, 2019–20, p. 3. https://rbidocs.rbi. org.in/rdocs/AnnualReport/PDFs/0RBIAR201920DA64F97C6E7B48848 E6DEA06D531BADF.PDF

16. Reserve Bank of India, Annual Report, 2020–21, p. 7. https://rbidocs.rbi. org.in/rdocs/AnnualReport/PDFs/0RBIAR202021_F49F9833694E84C16 AAD01BE48F53F6A2.PDF

17. PIB, Government of India, Cabinet Committee on Economic Affairs, 'Cabinet approves strategic disinvestment of CPSEs', 20 November 2019. https://pib.gov.in/PressReleasePage.aspx?PRID=1592540

18. PIB, Government of India, 'Cabinet approves "In Principle" strategic disinvestment of equity shareholding of Minerals & Metals Trading Corporation Limited, National Mineral Development Corporation, MECON and Bharat Heavy Electricals Ltd in Neelachal Ispat Nigam Limited. a JV Company with two Government of Odisha State PSUs', 8 January 2020, https://pib.gov.in/Pressreleaseshare.aspx?PRID=1598715

19. Government of India Ministry of Finance Lok Sabha Unstarred Question No: 1264 answered on: 10.02.2020 http://loksabhaph.nic.in/Questions/ QResult15.aspx?qref=12393&lsno=17

20. Nikhil Inamdar, 'Coronavirus lockdown: India jobless numbers cross 120 million in April 2020', 6 May 2020, BBC News, Mumbai www.bbc. com/news/world-asia-india-52559324

21. PIB, Government of India, 'Finance minister announces government reforms and enablers across seven sectors under Aatma Nirbhar Bharat Abhiyaan', 17 May 2020, https://pib.gov.in/PressReleasePage.aspx?PRID= 1624661

22. PIB, Government of India, 1 February 2021, https://pib.gov.in/ PressReleseDetailm.aspx?PRID=1693899

6 Big ticket privatisation and asset monetisation proposed in Fiscal 2022

Ambitious plans for privatisation in FY, 2021–22

While presenting the budget for 2021–22 on 1 February 2021, the Union Finance Minister Nirmala Sitharaman announced the disinvestment target of ₹ 1.75 lakh crore (₹ 1.75 trillion) for FY 2022. Disinvestments which could not be completed in 2020–21 namely BPCL, Air India, Shipping Corporation of India, Container Corporation of India, IDBI Bank, BEML, Pawan Hans, Neelachal Ispat Nigam limited among others were now slated for Fiscal 2022. The FM also announced that other than IDBI Bank, privatisation of two Public Sector Banks and one General Insurance company would be undertaken in the year 2021–22. Further, the government would bring the IPO of Life Insurance Corporation (LIC).

These were big ticket privatisations. The Chief Economic Advisor to the Government of India, K. V. Subramanian asserted that the disinvestment target of ₹ 1.75 lakh crore for 2021–22 was 'eminently achievable'. He said 'Of this, BPCL privatisation and LIC listing itself were important contributors. There are estimates suggesting ₹75,000–₹80,000 crore or even higher can just come from the privatisation of BPCL. LIC IPO could bring in ₹1 lakh crore approximately.'[1] Bloomberg reported that the government's 53% stake in the BPCL was valued at about ₹ 50,900 crore ($6.9 billion) based on 7 May 2021 closing price.[2]

Workers protest and Government Assurance

Worker unions protested against privatisation of banks and IPO in LIC. Public sector bank employees under the banner of the United Forum of Bank Unions, an umbrella organisation of nine trade unions, went on strike for two days from 15 March 2021. The unions feared that the privatisation of banks would lead to loss of employment. Employees

DOI: 10.4324/9781003262213-7

of LIC also protested on 18 March 2021 against the proposed IPO and enhancing FDI limit in insurance sector from 49% to 74%.

The Finance Minister, Nirmala Sitharaman during an interaction following her address to India Inc. at the Economic Times Awards for Corporate Excellence on 20 March 2021 said 'When we are speaking about privatisation, I do recognise that these units are in economic activities that are critical for the country. Privatisation is not going to end up as selling for closure. I am selling to continue to be in business because they aren't being run efficiently and we do not have money of the scale that is needed to invest,' She added that the government would ensure protection of rights and perquisites of workers of public sector units that are put up for privatisation.[3]

Thrust of Union Budget, 2021–22: New infrastructure

National Infrastructure Pipeline (NIP)

India's National Infrastructure Pipeline (NIP) Report was prepared in 2019 by the Task Force headed by Secretary, Department of Economic Affairs, Ministry of Finance. It envisages an infrastructure investment of ₹ 111 lakh crore over the five-year period (FY 2020–25). As estimated by the Report, traditional sources of capital are expected to finance 83–85% of the capital expenditure. About 15–17% of the aggregate outlay is expected to be met through innovative mechanisms such as asset recycling and monetisation, and new long-term initiatives such as Development Finance Institution (DFI). As per NIP, asset recycling and monetisation mechanism may finance around 5–6% of the aggregate capital expenditure under NIP.[4]

Three pronged strategy to raise resources for infrastructure financing

In the Union Budget 2021–22, a three-pronged strategy was laid out for raising resources to finance new infrastructure investments in the country. Firstly, by creating institutional structures through a new development finance institution (DFI); secondly, through a big thrust on asset monetisation; and thirdly by enhancing share of capital expenditure in central and state budgets.

Infrastructure financing – development finance institution. Infrastructure needs long-term debt financing. A professionally managed development financial institution is necessary to act as a provider, enabler, and catalyst for infrastructure financing. The Parliament passed the National Bank for Financing Infrastructure and Development (NBFID) Bill, 2021 that enabled the creation of a DFI – 'NBFID', as a corporate body with authorised share capital of ₹ 1 lakh crore. The central government's share in the entity is envisaged to remain above 26% (currently at 100%). The central government envisages to capitalise this DFI initially with ₹20,000 crore. The budget envisioned the DFI to have a lending portfolio of at least ₹ 5 lakh crore in three years' time.[5]

Also, FM stated that debt financing of InVITs and REITs by Foreign Portfolio Investors will be facilitated by making suitable amendments in the relevant legislations. This would ease access of finance to InVITS and REITs and augment funds for infrastructure and real estate sectors.

Asset monetisation. Monetising operating public infrastructure assets is a very important financing option for new infrastructure construction. A 'National Monetization Pipeline' of potential brownfield infrastructure assets will be launched. An asset monetisation dashboard will also be created for tracking the progress and to provide visibility to investors. Some important measures in the direction of monetisation are:[6]

a. National Highways Authority of India and PGCIL each have sponsored one InVIT that will attract international and domestic institutional investors. Five operational roads with an estimated enterprise value of ₹5,000 crores are being transferred to the NHAI InVIT. Similarily, transmission assets of a value of ₹7,000 crores will be transferred to the PGCIL InVIT.

b. Railways will monetise Dedicated Freight Corridor assets for operations and maintenance, after commissioning.

c. The next lot of airports will be monetised for operations and management concession.

d. Other core infrastructure assets that will be rolled out under the Asset Monetisation Programme are: (i) NHAI Operational Toll Roads (ii) transmission assets of PGCIL (iii) oil and gas pipelines of GAIL, IOCL, and HPCL (iv) AAI Airports in Tier II and III cities, (v) other railway infrastructure assets, (vi) warehousing assets of CPSEs such as Central Warehousing Corporation and NAFED among others, and (vii) sports stadiums.

Having said that in the Union Budget 2021–22, the Finance Minister announced the National Monetisation Pipeline on 23 August 2021.

Enhancing share of capital expenditure in state budgets. Central Government launched a 'Scheme for Special Assistance to States for Capital Expenditure' as part of 'Aatma Nirbhar Bharat' package in September 2020. Union Budget 2021–22 further announced that the

Centre would take measures to incentivise states to spend more on infrastructure and to incentivise disinvestment of their public sector enterprises. As an incentive for asset monetisation, additional allocation equivalent to 33% of value of assets realised is envisaged to be deposited in state consolidated funds or in account of state public sector enterprises owning the assets. Funds provided to the states under the scheme shall be used for new and ongoing capital projects, and may also be used for settling pending bills in ongoing capital projects.[7]

National Monetisation Pipeline (NMP)

National Monetisation Pipeline (NMP) of potential brownfield infrastructure assets was prepared by the NITI Aayog. NMP has been planned to be co-terminus with the remaining four-year period of the National Infrastructure Pipeline (NIP) from FY 22 to FY25.The Report has been organised into two volumes. Volume I is structured as a guidance book, detailing the conceptual approaches and potential models for asset monetisation. Volume II is the actual roadmap for monetisation, including the pipeline of core infrastructure assets under central government line ministries and CPSEs in infrastructure sectors.[8]

According to the preface to the NITI Aayog Report, Volume I (pp. iii–iv) 'Asset monetisation is based on the philosophy of "creation through monetisation". It will tap institutional investment and long term patient capital into stable mature assets in turn generating financial resources for new infrastructure. This will enable economic growth, generating opportunities and better prospects for country's youth.'

Key features of National Monetisation Pipeline

- Assets Monetisation entails a limited period license/lease of an asset, owned by the government or a pubic authority to a private sector entity for an upfront or periodic consideration (NITI Aayog, National Monetisation Pipeline: Volume I, p. 5).
- Assets which are central to the business objectives of a public entity and are being utilised for delivering infrastructure services to public/ users have been categorised as Core Assets for the purpose of monetisation (NITI Aayog, National Monetisation Pipeline:Volume I, p. 10).
- Monetisation through disinvestment and monetisation of non-core assets (such as lands, buildings, and pure play real estate assets) have not been included in the NMP (NITI Aayog, National Monetisation Pipeline: Volume II, p. 6).

- Monetisation value is only an indicative high level estimate based on thumb rule estimates, The actual monetisation value will be determined based on detailed valuation or feasibility studies. The actual realisation (whether by way of accruals or by way of private investment) will depend on various factors such as transaction timing, economic scenario, available capital, and investor interest. (NITI Aayog, National Monetisation Pipeline: Volume II, pp. 7–8).

NIP and NMP, together, are envisaged to give a comprehensive view on greenfield and brownfield investment avenues in Infrastructure.

Details of NMP[9]

The government is looking to monetise to get about ₹ 6 lakh crore, i.e. ₹6 trillion about $81 billion at the exchange rate of $1 = 74.16 rupees) to partly fund its ambitious infrastructure projects over four years ending 2024–25. About ₹ 88,000 crore will be realised through asset monetisation in the current financial year, 2021–22. The FM clarified that the ownership of all these assets would remain with the government, and there would be a mandatory hand-back of assets after a certain time period. 'So, the government is not selling away these assets,' she said.

The National Monetisation Pipeline (NMP) will constitute 14% of the Centre's share of ₹ 43.29 trillion in the National Infrastructure Pipeline (NIP). Global players such as Blackstone, Blackrock, and Macquarie have shown interest in participating in the monetisation process.

The plan covers 20 asset classes spread over 12 line ministries and departments. The top three sectors by value are roads (₹ 1.6 trillion), railways (₹ 1.5 trillion), and power (₹ 85,032 crore). The NMP does not include land, but lays the road map for monetising brownfield projects where investments have already been made, where a completed asset is languishing or which is not fully utilised, Sitharaman said. 'By bringing private participation, we will be able to monetise these assets better and resources obtained through monetisation would be used for putting further investment into infrastructure building,' she added.

Sitharaman said the asset monetisation programme is aimed at tapping private sector investment for new infrastructure creation, and is necessary for creating employment opportunities, enabling high economic growth, and seamlessly integrating the rural and semi-urban areas for the overall public welfare. Contractual partnerships for the execution of the asset monetisation pipeline will be with key performance indicators and performance standards, she said. 'They are all de-risked assets, and the value from the consideration and private investment which will come into maintaining it and optimally utilising it will generate greater value and unlock resources for the economy,' she said.

Sector wise details of assets over a four-year period (FY 2022 to FY 2025)[10]

In the roads sector, about 26,700 km stretch would be monetised to mop up around ₹1.6 trillion. The National Highway Authority of India (NHAI) and the Ministry of Road Transport and Highways will drive this through the toll, operate, and transfer (TOT) and Infrastructure Investment Trusts (InvITs) models.

The plan includes monetising power transmission lines of 28,609 ckt km to garner ₹ 45,200 crore. These will be driven by Power Grid Corporation. Monetisation of hydro and solar power generation assets of 6 Gw would help the government realise ₹ 39,832 crore, and would be undertaken by National Thermal Power Corporation, National Hydroelectric Power Corporation, and NLC India. Natural gas pipeline of 8,154 km would be monetised by GAIL with an indicative value of ₹ 24,462 crore.

The plan also includes petroleum product pipelines of 3,930 km to be monetised by Indian Oil Corporation, Hindustan Petroleum Corporation and the Ministry of Petroleum and Natural Gas. This would help in realising ₹ 22,503 crore through public–private partnerships (PPPs) and InvITs.

The government will also monetise warehousing assets of 210 lakh MT to realise ₹ 28,900 crore. These assets are currently owned by Food Corporation of India and the Department of Food and Public Distribution.

For railways, the plan is to monetise railway stations, passenger trains, good sheds, Konkan Railway, Hill Railways, dedicated freight corridor, and railway stadiums to get ₹ 1.52 trillion. In the telecom sector, 2.86 lakh km fibre and 14,917 towers of BSNL and MTNL are planned to be monetised that will help in realising about ₹ 35,100 crore.

In aviation, the plan is to sell 25 airports, and reduce the Airport Authority of India's (AAI) stake in existing airports such as Delhi, Mumbai, Hyderabad, and Bangalore. This would garner proceeds of ₹ 20,782 crore.

In the shipping sector, 31 projects in nine major ports would be monetised to realise ₹ 12,828 crore.

In the coal mining sector, 160 projects have been identified involving a value of ₹28,747 crore. In sports, two national stadiums and two regional centres would be monetised to get a value of ₹11,450 crore. In urban real estate, redevelopment of colonies and hospitality assets worth ₹ 15,000 crore will be monetised.

The assets and transactions identified under the NMP are expected to be rolled out through a range of instruments. These include direct contractual instruments such as public private partnership concessions and capital market instruments such as Infrastructure Investment Trusts (InvIT) among others. The choice of instrument will be determined by the sector, nature of asset, timing of transactions (including market considerations), target investor profile and the level of operational/investment control envisaged to be retained by the asset owner etc. The various potential models for brownfield PPP of existing infrastructure assets owned by public sector entities include: Operate Maintain Transfer (OMT), Operate Maintain Develop (OMD), Toll Operate Transfer (TOT) in Roads, and Operation Management Development Agreement (OMDA) in Airports.

Consolidated Pipeline

The total indicative value of NMP for Core Assets of Central Government has been estimated at about ₹ 6.0 lakh crore over the four-year period, FY22–25 The estimated value corresponds to about 5.4% of the total infrastructure investment envisaged under the NIP which is around ₹ 111 lakh crore and is 14% of the proposed outlay for Centre (₹ 43 lakh crore). This pipeline of assets has been phased out over a four-year period starting FY 2022 up till FY 2025.

The overall sectoral contribution from FY 2022 to FY 2025 is given in Table 6.1.

As can be observed, the top five sectors (by estimated value) capture about 83% of the aggregate pipeline value. These top five sectors include: Roads (27%) followed by Railways (25%), Power (15%), Oil & Gas Pipelines (8%), and Telecom (6%). Roads and Railways together contribute about 52% of the total NMP value.

Indicative value of monetisation pipeline for FY 2022 to FY 2025 is tabulated in Table 6.2.

Risks and challenges in asset monetisation

In past, the asset monetisation model in India has had a mixed track record with investors. In the road sector government has already garnered ₹170 billion, but India's plan to allow private players to operate some trains did not generate as much interest as expected due to regulations and contract enforcement requirements.

Table 6.1 Sector wise monetisation pipeline over FY 2022−2025

Sector	Indicative value (% share in NMP)	Assets for monetisation
ROADS	₹160,200 crore (27%)	26,700 km − Marque Project: NHAI's Infrastructure Investment Trust (InvIT)
RAILWAYS	₹152,496 crore (26%)	400 railway stations (5.5% of stations), 90 passenger trains (5% of total trains) Railway track (1400 km), Konkan Railways (741 km), Hill Railways (4 Nos. 244 km route), 265 Good-sheds, 15 Railway stadiums and selected Railway Colonies, Dedicated Freight Corridor (DFC) track -673 km (20 % of total DFC network. Note: Bidding for 150 private passenger trains is underway.
POWER TRANSMISSION	₹45,200 crore (8%)	Marquee Project: Monetisation of transmission assets of POWERGRID through Infrastructure Investment Trust (InvIT)
POWER GENERATION	₹39,832 crore (7%)	6 GW (3.5 GW Hydro and 2.5 GW RE)
TELECOM	₹35,100 crore (6%)	2.86 lakh km of Bharatnet Fiber, 14917 Nos of BSNL and MTNL towers.
NATURAL GAS PIPELINE	₹24,462crore (4%)	8,154 km
PETROLEUM, PETROLEUM PRODUCT PIPELINES & OTHER ASSETS	₹22,503 crore (4%)	3,930 km
WAREHOUSING	₹28,900 crore (5%)	210 lakh metric ton (LMT)[175 LMT of FCI and 35 LMT of CWC]
MINING ASSETS – COAL MINING & MINERAL MINING	₹28,747 crore (5%)	Coal mining 160 projects,

(*continued*)

Table 6.1 Cont.

Sector	Indicative value (% share in NMP)	Assets for monetisation
AIRPORTS	₹ 20,782 crore (4%)	25 number of AAI airports considered for monetisation. During FY 2022, 6 airports identified for monetisation by clubbing with smaller airports. Divestment of residual stake in 4 airports – Mumbai (26%), Delhi (26%), Hyderabad (13%), and Bangalore (13%).
PORTS	₹12,828 crore (2%)	31 Projects in 9 of the 12 major ports in the country.
SPORTS STADIA	₹11,450 crore (2%)	2 National Stadiums (JLN stadium and one more), and 2 regional centers (Bangalore, & Zirakpur).
URBAN REAL ESTATE ASSETS- HOUSING REDEVELOPMENT	₹15,000 crore (2.5%)	NMP estimates investment required is of ₹32,276 crore for redevelopment of 7 General Pool Residential accommodation colonies in Delhi, and ₹15000 crore for development of residential / commercial units on 240 acre land in Ghitrorni (Delhi). 8 ITDC Hotels of ITDC has been approved under NMP: Hotel Pondichery, Puducherry; Hotel Kalinga, Bhubaneswar; Hotel Ranchi, Ranchi; Hotel Nilachal, Puri; Hotel Anandpur Sahib, Rupnagar; Hotel Samrat, New Delhi; Hotel Ashok, New Delhi; Hotel Jammu,
GRAND TOTAL (FY 2022 to 2025)	**₹5,97,500 crore (about ₹6 lakh cr)**	

Source: Created by author based on NITI Aayog, National Monetisation Pipeline, Volume II: Asset Pipeline, www.niti.gov.in/sites/default/files/2021-08/Vol_2_NATIONAL_ MONETISATION_PIPELINE_23_Aug_2021.pdf

Table 6.2 Indicative value of monetisation for FY 2022–2025

S. No,	Financial year	Indicative value of monetisation
1	2021-22	₹ 88,190 crore
2	2022-23	₹ 162,422 crore
3	2023-24	₹179,544 crore
4	2024-25	₹167,345 crore
	FY 2022 to 2025 (4 years)	**₹597,501crore**

Source: Created by author based on NITI Aayog, National Monetisation Pipeline, Volume II: Asset Pipeline, p.15, www.niti.gov.in/sites/default/files/2021-08/Vol_2_NATIONAL_MONETISATION_PIPELINE_23_Aug_2021.pdf

It is important that the funds realised through monetisation of assets are spent on creation of new infrastructure, and not in revenue expenditure. Once the asset monetisation realisations are put in Consolidated Fund of India, it is obfuscate whether the funds are used for capital or revenue expenditure. A separate mechanism to ensure that such funds are utilised for the avowed purpose should be ensured.

Undertaking asset monetisation at such a gigantic scale when India is facing challenges of Covid-19 pandemic, endemic poverty, economic slowdown, social polarisation, geopolitical chaos, and global warming, raises questions about its timing in 2021–22 for a four years period till 2024–25. The next general elections for the federal government are due in 2024–25 (before May 2024).

The economists have spoken about the risks involved in asset monetisation model, such as concentration of wealth in the hands of few, increasing inequalities, lower emphasis on public welfare, higher user charges, asset stripping, and capture of state as happened in early 1990s in Russia.

Vikram Singh Mehta, former CEO Shell India and Executive Chairman of Brookings India, while writing in *The Indian Express* (6 September 2021) said NMP is designed to attract deep pocketed financial institutions (PE firms) and industrial conglomerates. This is because the valuations are so high that few other entities will have the resources or the risk carrying capacity to respond. This will be deepening the concentration of capital and existing inequalities. Further, NMP has been conceptualised around the metric of financial value. The assets are leased (not sold) at appropriately discounted lease charges. The focus of the investors is understandably to recover their upfront payments plus earn their threshold revenue return within stipulated lease period. This model which looks at public utility assets through the narrow lens of finance only is problematic. It underrates assets potential contribution to public welfare.[11]

Once control is out of the government's hands for decades, the public will worry about higher user charges by operators of roads, railways, airports, power grids, and gas pipelines. In past, Singapore had to nationalise its suburban trains and signalling systems because the main private operator had underinvested in maintenance, leading to frequent breakdowns and stranded, angry passengers. In New South Wales, where electricity prices doubled in five years after poles and wires were privatised, the government had to step in with an Energy Affordability Package to lower the burden on consumers.[12]

Australian Competition and Consumer Commission (ACCC) Chairman Rod Sims while speaking at the 2021 ACCC/AER Regulatory Conference emphasised need to either avoid monopolies, or if not, then regulate them to prevent costs to the economy arising from unfettered use of their market power.[13]

Kaushik Basu, professor at Cornell University and formerly Chief Economist of the World Bank (2012 to 2016) and Chief Economic Adviser to the Government of India (2009 to 2012) said in an interview to NDTV on 27 August 2021 that instead of leasing, limited sale by carefully designed auctions should be undertaken. Selling would get the government higher price than leasing. Auctions can be designed by economists to get right price. Citing a case during his tenure in India as CEA, he said at the time of spectrum auction, the bureaucrats estimated the value as $7 billion, but economists designed the auction and the government got $15 billion. He added that the present asset monetisation model would result in assets being captured by a few big corporate. There is a genuine risk of capture and asset stripping like what happened in 1990s in Russia under Boris Yeltsin, when oligarchs created a stranglehold on the economy. He said, the government of any political party should be aware of this risk. Though USA has mature antitrust laws, but is still grappling with issues of monopolisation and India has relatively new such regulatory laws.[14]

The private sector needs space to run things efficiently but there is also a need for a welfare state during the period of low consumption and job loss in the pandemic. Finding the right balance between public and private interests is thus of critical importance.

Plans to sell PSUs land

It was reported in *Business Standard* on 3 September 2021 that Union Government is planning to sell land parcels worth more than ₹600 crore in some public sector undertakings through its new online bidding plateform. This initiative will be managed by the Department of Investment and Public Asset Management (DIPAM). Unlike the NMP, the ownership of assets will be transferred in the case of PSU land sale. In first go, assets which are free from any litigation would be sold. The land assets of BSNL, MTNL, BEML, and Shipping Corporation of India among others are on block.[15]

Efficiency scrutinies to optimise resources

Other than raising resources by the usual methods, the government have to optimise use of resources and avoid infructous expenditure. A rupee saved is a rupee earned. To bring fiscal prudence, and efficiency in government, it is suggested that all ministries/ departments should undertake a comprehensive efficiency scrutiny analysis of their organisations/ programmes. Such an analysis would bring out what an organisation has been doing historically oblivious to the present day need. There is a lot of scope to raise resources by monetisation of lands in Ministry of Defence. A study was conducted way back on optimisation of army lands. Estimates Committee (1991–92), Parliament of India notes of it.[16] The Report recommended three decades back closure of military farms. Military farms had a role when established but with the 'white revolution', milk was available in plenty throughout the country from few decades. But the 39 farms holding about 20,000 acres of land were closed down only on 31 March 2021.[17] Another organisation, which was considered by the optimisation of Army Lands Committee was Remount and Veterinary Corps, holding thousands of acres of land in its equine breeding studs to raise horses and mules for the India Army. A bold step was taken by the government in September 2021 to dissolve the over 200-year-old Ordnance Factory Board , a departmental undertaking under Ministry of Defence , and transfer its assets (41 ordnance factories) and employees to 7 new public sector undertakings.

The concept of efficiency scrutiny is not new. In UK, such an Efficiency Unit was established in 1979 after Margaret Thatcher took office as Prime Minister. The purpose of scrutinies was to examine a specific policy, activity or function with a view to savings or increased effectiveness and to questioning all aspects of the work normally taken for granted. This was to be carried out by the Departments by a small group (two to five members) of individuals whose experience meant they were concerned with, but not necessarily from, the area being looked at.[18]

Specific cases of big ticket privatisations

In the next six chapters we will discuss the big ticket privatisations which government is focusing on either to get money or stop losing further money – the top three loss making CPSEs (Air India, BSNL & MTNL), *Maharatna* BPCL listed in top ten profit making CPSEs (*Maharatna* status gives more autonomy), and privatising airports, public sector banks, and disinvestment in LIC. It is a mixed bag of one of the most profitable CPSE and most loss making CPSEs.

References

1. The Hindu (2021). 'Disinvestment goal achievable: LIC IPO to fetch ₹ 1 lakh crore: CEA', 27 March. www.thehindu.com/business/Economy/divestment-goal-achievable-lic-ipo-to-fetch-1-lakh-crore-cea/article34179185.ece

2. Baiju Kalesh and Debit Chakraborty (2021). 'Govt gives bidders data access for $7-billion Bharat Petroleum Sale', *Bloomberg*, 7 May, accessed 26 May 2021, www.bloomberg.com/news/articles/2021-05-07/india-said-to-give-bidders-data-access-for-7-billion-bpcl-sale

3. Times of India, 'FM promises to protect rights and perks of workers of privatised PSUs', 21 March 2021,p. 1. https://timesofindia.indiatimes.com/business/india-business/fm-promises-to-protect-rights-and-perks-of-workers-of-privatised-psus/articleshow/81609720.cms

4. NITI Aayog, National Monetisation Pipeline, Volume I, p. 3: Monetisation Guidebook. www.niti.gov.in/sites/default/files/2021-08/Vol_I_NATIONAL_MONETISATION_PIPELINE_23_Aug_2021.pdf

5. NITI Aayog, National Monetisation Pipeline, Volume II: Asset Pipeline, p. 3 www.niti.gov.in/sites/default/files/2021-08/Vol_2_NATIONAL_MONETISATION_PIPELINE_23_Aug_2021.pdf

6. Government of India, Budget 2021–2022, Finance Minister Speech, February 1,2021,para 47. www.indiabudget.gov.in/doc/budget_speech.pdf

7. NITI Aayog, National Monetisation Pipeline, Volume II: Asset Pipeline, pp. 3–4. www.niti.gov.in/sites/default/files/2021-08/Vol_2_NATIONAL_MONETISATION_PIPELINE_23_Aug_2021.pdf

8. NITI Aayog, National Monetisation Pipeline, Volume I: Monetisation Guidebook. www.niti.gov.in/sites/default/files/2021-08/Vol_I_NATIONAL_MONETISATION_PIPELINE_23_Aug_2021.pdf, and NITI Aayog, National Monetisation Pipeline, Volume II: Asset Pipeline, www.niti.gov.in/sites/default/files/2021-08/Vol_2_NATIONAL_MONETISATION_PIPELINE_23_Aug_2021.pdf

9. Nikunj Ohri and Indivjal Dhasmana, 'FM announces plan to monetise assets, realise Rs 6 trillion till 2024–25', *Business Standard*, New Delhi, 23 August 2021. www.business-standard.com/article/economy-policy/fm-announces-plan-to-monetise-assets-realise-rs-6-trillion-till-2024-25-121082300923_1.html

10. NITI Aayog, National Monetisation Pipeline, Volume II: Asset Pipeline, www.niti.gov.in/sites/default/files/2021-08/Vol_2_NATIONAL_MONETISATION_PIPELINE_23_Aug_2021.pdf

11. Vikram Singh Mehta, 'On assets, a narrow view', *The Indian Express*, 6 September 2021, p. 11. https://indianexpress.com/article/opinion/columns/national-monetisation-pipeline-nirmala-sitharaman-private-public-investment-7490917/

12. Andy Mukherjee, 'Not just tycoons, India's asset monetisation plan must treat all fairly', *Bloomberg Opinion*, 25 August 2021. www.business-standard.com/article/economy-policy/not-just-tycoons-india-s-asset-monetisation-plan-must-treat-all-fairly-121082500102_1.html

13. Rod Sims,'Privatise for efficiency, or not at all', Australian Competition & Consumer Commission, 30 July 2021, www.accc.gov.au/media-release/privatise-for-efficiency-or-not-at-all

14. NDTV, 27 August 2021, www.ndtv.com/video/business/the-big-fight/leasing-out-assets-worst-option-kaushik-basu-tells-ndtv-599625

15. Nikunj Ohri, 'Centre plans PSU landsale via e-bidding', *Business Standard*, 4 September 2001, p. 1.

16. Ninth Report Estimates Committee (1991–92) (Tenth Lok Sabha) Ministry of Defence, 'Defence lands and land use policy', Lok Sabha Secretariat, New Delhi. Para 1.6 (p. 7), and Para 2.22 (p. 30). https://eparlib.nic.in/handle/123456789/761351?view_type=search

17. Man Amar Singh Chhina, 'Explained: Why has the Indian Army shut down its Military Farms Service?', *Indian Express*, 8 April 2021, https://indianexpress.com/article/explained/indian-army-military-farms-service-7254643/

18. Catherine Haddon. 'Reforming the civil service, The Efficiency Unit in the early 1980s and the 1987 next steps', Institute for Government, www.instituteforgovernment.org.uk/sites/default/files/publications/Efficiency%20Unit%20and%20Next%20Steps.pdf

7 Privatisation of Air India

Evolution of Air India and Indian Airlines

Tata Airlines was set up on 15 October 1932 as the first scheduled air-mail service in India. In July 1946, the company was converted into a public limited company and renamed as Air-India. By the end of 1947, Air India International was launched for international services, with the participation of the Government of India. In 1952, the Planning Commission recommended nationalisation of the air transport industry. Nationalisation was effected on 1 August 1953 with the creation of two corporations, viz Air India for international services (as the nation's flag carrier) and Indian Airlines for domestic services.

Past efforts to restructure airlines and merger

Vijay Kelkar Committee, 1997

Due to mounting financial distress, many efforts were made to restructure or disinvest Air India and Indian Airlines. In 1997, the United Front Government had appointed Vijay Kelkar Committee on restructuring of Indian Airlines and Air India. In a written answer to Lok Sabha Question 6314 on 15 May 1997, the then Minister of Civil Aviation, C. M. Ibrahim informed that the Kelkar Committee had proposed a multi pronged two phase strategy to help the Indian Airlines.[1] However, the Government did not pursue to get report on Air India, as noted by the Department-Related Parliamentary Standing Committee on Transport & Tourism at its meeting held in June 2000.

Disinvestment Commission

In September 1996, the Government had included Air India in the first list of CPSEs given to the Disinvestment Commission constituted in

DOI: 10.4324/9781003262213-8

August 1996. The Commission in August 1998 (Report VIII) noted that AI has been operating at negative spread from FY 1996 onwards. Its share of traffic to and from India has fallen and it has been unable to attract high yielding first/business class passengers. The main recommendations of the Commission was infusion of ₹1,000 crore as equity for expansion and modernisation of Air India, followed by strategic sale by issue of new shares reducing Government holding to 60%, and then subsequent offer of sale of 20% to domestic investors.[2]

NDA Government effort (March 1998–May 2004)

During the National Democratic Alliance (NDA) I Government led by Atal Bihari Vajpayee (March 1998 to May 2004), the Cabinet Committee on Disinvestment (CCD) on 26 May 2000 approved in principle bringing down the equity of the Government of India in Air India to 40% through a process of disinvestment by sale of 40% of equity to a strategic partner, up to 10% to employees and the balance by sale to financial institutions and/or on the share market. It was further decided that in the event of the strategic partner being a joint venture with an element of foreign holding, the arrangement should be such as would limit foreign holding in Air India to a maximum of 26% of the total equity.[3]

The Department-Related Parliamentary Standing Committee on Transport & Tourism at its meeting held on 27 June 2000 expressed anguish at the Government's failure to take any steps for restructuring of Air India or to arrest the decline in the fortunes of Air India.[3] It observed that while the Government received the report in respect of India Airlines, it did not pursue getting the report on Air India. The Committee noted that the Government did not agree to provide equity of ₹1,000 crores as recommended by the Disinvestment Commission. Even ₹750 crores as required by Air India to make a turn around have not been provided.[3]

The Committee further noted with anguish that the Government had been virtually ignoring the assets of Air India built over a period of nearly 50 years. It observed that without taking any concrete and effective steps for the revival of Air India, the Government had straightaway decided to go in for disinvestment of Air India. Air India had been a profit making undertaking for quite a long period. The Committee felt that the Government's decision to go in for disinvestment of Air India might have affected the morale of the employees and management of Air India which led to the deterioration in the functioning of Air India (Para 17).[3] The Committee also strongly disapproved the idea of the Government to offer 26% equity and the management control of Air India to the foreign strategic partner. The Committee, recommended that in order to protect the sovereign rights of the country, the Government should reconsider the proposal regarding allowing 26% of the equity to the foreign partner and restrict the same to 25% so that the de-facto control of the management of Air India remained with Indian nationals (Para 19). The Committee also discussed as to what would be the position of the Government vis-à-vis Air India when there is a situation like war, natural calamity, emergency, etc. The Committee wanted to know how the Government would ensure the synchronisation of the national/social objectives of the Government/Air India as a national carrier vis-à-vis the commercial objectives of management of Air India after the proposed disinvestment (Para 21).[3]

Finally, the Committee was of the view that disinvestment of Air India should not appear to be desperate and a distress sale. Proper guidelines should be formulated and announced framing the parameters for the Global Advisor (Para 25).[3]

Merger of Air India and Indian Airlines in 2007

The Government decided to merge Air India and Indian Airlines into a new company National Aviation Company of India Limited (NACIL) which was incorporated on 30 March 2007. The merger became effective on 27 August 2007 when all assets, liabilities, and obligations of both these companies were taken over by NACIL, and Air India Limited and Indian Airlines Limited were dissolved without being wound up. The entire paid-up share capital of newly formed NACIL was held by the Government of India. On 24 November 2010 name of the Company was changed from 'NACIL' to 'Air India Limited'.[4]

Ashwani Lohani, Chairman and Managing Director, Air India in an interview with *The Economic Times* published on 1 July 2016 said that the merger led to Air India's downfall. There were many differences between the two companies in terms of work culture, areas of operation, compensation, working conditions, entitlements etc. The merger resulted in massive discontent and frustration amongst the staff. The subsequent demerger of ground handling and engineering companies added to the problems.[5]

Air India's total accumulated loss post merger from 2007–08 till 2015–16 was ₹ 49,218 crores.[6]

Mounting losses and inefficiency

There were reports in the media regarding sorry state of affairs in Air India. *The New York Times*, on 26 May 2011 carried a story 'Losses

Rise as Pilots and Passengers Forsake State-Owned Air India'. It wrote, 'Instead of throwing good money after bad, the time has come to stand up and say: yes, Air India must be shut down'. The Center for Asia Pacific Aviation, a research group in Sydney, Australia, singled out Air India as an example of government mismanagement. 'I feel like a woman with 1,000 husbands,' one male Air India executive complained, referring to the constant demands from government officials.[7] However, India's then civil aviation minister, vowed in an interview on 25 May 2011, not to close or sell the airline.

Financials of Air India, FY 2015 to 2019

According to the Public Enterprises Survey, 2018–19, Air India had the second highest loss amongst the Central Public Sector Enterprises (CPSEs) and accounted for more than a quarter of losses (26.8%) of all loss-making CPSEs in that year. It has been the second highest loss making CPSE since 2014–15. Air India incurred a net loss of about ₹ 2,570 crore in the first quarter of 2020–21 as compared to a net loss of ₹ 785 crore sustained in the corresponding period a year ago. Profit & Loss of Air India from FY 2015 to FY 2019 is tabulated in Table 7.1.

Monetisation of Air India assets had started from FY 2013

Cabinet Committee on Economic Affairs (CCEA) in its meeting on 12 April 2012 approved the Turn Around Plan (TAP) and Financial Restructuring Plan (FRP) for Air India. It had also approved Monetisation of Real Estate Assets in Air India to the tune of ₹.5000 crore over the next 10 years period with the annual target of ₹500 crore from the Financial Year 2013 onwards. The then Minister for Civil Aviation Jayant Sinha informed Parliament in a written reply to the Lok Sabha on 20 December 2018, that Air India had realised ₹ 724 crore through its asset monetisation programme as well as from space rentals. Of this ₹ 410 crore was on account of sale of non-core assets and ₹ 314 crore rental income.[8]

Efforts for strategic disinvestment/privatisaion in 2017–18

In May 2017, NITI Aayog submitted its recommendations (Fourth Tranche) on Strategic Disinvestment of the Central Public Sector Enterprises. The Aayog recommended disinvestment of Air India because of its fragile finances. AI has been incurring continuous losses and has huge accumulated losses. It is incurring a cash deficit

Table 7.1 Air India – profit and loss for FY 2015 to FY 2019 (In million of ₹)*

S.No.	Details	Financial Year				
		2014–15	2015–16	2016–17	2017–18	2018–19
	REVENUE					
1	Operating revenue	198,017	202,108	218,217	229,481	255,088
2	Other income	8,115	3,995	3,700	8,968	9,218
3	**Total revenue**	206,132	206,103	221,971	238,449	264,306
	EXPENSES					
4	Fuel expenses	84,491	58,454	63,453	73,627	100,345
5	Employee expenses	24,666	23,455	25,646	29,464	30,052
6	Other operating expenses	69,809	72,704	81,098	86,549	100,188
7	Other expenses	10,761	10,159	14,209	15,026	14,798
8	**Total expenses**	189,727	164,772	184,406	204,666	245,383
9	EBITDA (excluding other income)[a]	(-)2,693	25,598	15,312	1,264	(-)21,221
10	EBITDA (including other income)	5,422	29,593	19,012	10,232	(-)12,003
11	EBIT[b]	(-)13,786	(-)10,915	2,989	(-)6,442	(-)27,882
12	PBT[c]/PAT[d]	(-)58,599	(-)38,368	(-)64,529	(-) 53,482	(-)85,563
13	PBT/PAT Margin[e]	(-)28%	(-)19%	(-)29%	(-)22%	(-)32%

Source: 'Preliminary Information Memorandum (PIM) For Strategic Disinvestment of Air India', issued on 27 January 2020, p. 47, accessed 26 May 2021, https://indiainvestmentgrid.gov.in/assets/iigNew2/pdf/AirIndia/AI_Preliminary_IM_Jan2020.pdf

Notes:

* A million is ten lakh in Indian system of counting, and a crore is ten million.
a EBITDA: Earnings Before Interest, Tax, Depreciation and Amortisation.
b EBIT, Earnings Before Interest and Tax.
c PBT, Profit Before Tax.
d PAT, Profit After Tax.
e PBT Margin is Pretax profit margin.. The percentage ratio is calculated by deducting all expenses except for taxes, found in the income before taxes figure, dividing it by sales and then multiplying the resulting number by 100. PAT Margin is a financial performance ratio calculated by dividing net income by net sales.

of around ₹ 200–250 crore per month mainly on account of huge debt service burden. The losses can also be attributable to the decision of merger taken in 2007 wherein two very different organisations with dissimilar equipment and human resources practices were intended to be merged. Further, financial support in a mature and competitive aviation market would not be the best use of scarce financial resources of the Government. The Cabinet Committee on Economic Affairs (CCEA), in its meeting held in June 2017, gave in-principle approval for considering strategic disinvestment of Air India and its five subsidiaries.[9]

On 29 March 2018, the Government issued advertisement to sell 76% of Air India along with low-fare subsidiary Air India Express and a 50% stake in AISATS, a ground handling joint venture with Singapore Airport Terminal Services (SATS), as a single entity along with most of the national carrier's debt. A number of other conditions were also put, such as buyer was supposed to take on a debt worth ₹ 33,392 crore, bidder had to be profitable in at least three years of the previous five years, the lead member in a consortium needed to own at least 51% and the threshold for other members was 20%.[10]

Though InterGlobe Aviation Ltd – which operates India's largest domestic carrier IndiGo had shown interest in buying the government's entire stake in Air India but later backed out. IndiGo co-founder Rakesh Gangwal said, a joint venture or a joint ownership with the government is at best 'a very very difficult proposition and we would not go down that path'.[11] Ultimately, the Government of India did not receive any bid for this offer.

Renewed efforts to privatise Air India in 2020

The Minister for Civil Aviation Hardeep Singh Puri, informed media on 27 January 2020 that the newly constituted Air India Specific Alternative Mechanism (AISAM) headed by the Union Home Minister and comprising of Union Ministers of Commerce & Industry, Finance & Corporate Affairs and Civil Aviation, as members, has approved the release of the Preliminary Information Memorandum (PIM) for inviting Expression of Interest (EOI) from the Interested Bidders (IBs) for Strategic Disinvestment of Air India. He informed that the Government had released the PIM for seeking EOI for strategic disinvestment of Air India.[12]

The Civil Aviation Minister said that even after infusion of about ₹ 30,500 crore as per Turn Around Plan (TRP) since 2012, Air India has been running into losses year after year. Due to its accumulated debt of about ₹ 60,000 crore, its financial position is in a very fragile condition. A few of the key decisive parameters in the current PIM include: Transfer of management control and sale of 100% shares of Air India along with Air India's 100% stake in its subsidiary, Air India Express Limited, and 50% stake in joint venture, AISATS. Freezing of Debt in Air India at ₹ 23,286.50 crore which is approximately equivalent to the Written Down Value (WDV) of combined assets of Air India and Air India Express. The liabilities to be retained in Air India will be equal to certain current and non-current assets. Considering the combined figures as on 31 March 2019 the liabilities retained would be ₹ 8771.5 crore. The remaining debt and liabilities of Air India and Air India Express will be allocated to SPV (Air India Assets Holding Limited). The last date to submit EoI was 17 March 2020.

However, subsequently number of changes was made in the bid. The important change was lowering of debt amount a prospective buyer will have to take on. While in 2018, the buyer was supposed to take on a debt worth ₹ 33,392 crore, now it was about ₹23,286.50 crore. Also, buyer eligibility criteria was eased and the minimum shareholding requirement, too, was reduced. In October 2020, with the pandemic hitting the potential bidders, the government sweetened the deal further by allowing prospective bidders the flexibility to decide the level of debt they wish to take on along with the loss-laden airline.[13]

The government resolve to go ahead with privatisation was clear when the Civil Aviation Minister stated on 15 September 2020 that 'Air India must be privatised or it will close down'.[14] The issue is whether Air India has become a victim of its internal mismanagement or government's inept decisions, or both.

At the time of issue of PIM in January 2020, the last date to submit Expression of Interest (EOI) was 17 March 2020 which was extended multiple times, and finally the last date was 14 December 2020. The Secretary, Department of Investment and Public Asset Management tweeted on 14 December 2020, that 'multiple expressions of interest have been received for strategic disinvestment of Air India'. Later, Interups, a United States based fund who had earlier shown interest pulled out. In March 2021, the Air India employees consortium was informed that they did not fulfil eligibility criteria. According to media, Tata Group was the frontrunner. Tata already operates two airlines in India – full-service carrier Vistara, which is in partnership with Singapore Airlines, and budget airline Air Asia India along with Malaysia's Air Asia Group.

Arindam Majumdar wrote in *Business Standard*, in 4 February 2021 issue that the government is expecting to fetch around ₹ 15,000 crore from the sale of Air India, its subsidiary Air India Express and AISATS, according to officials and bankers involved in the divestment process.. The government had appointed RBSA Advisors for valuation of reserve price of Air India.[15]

New spanners in Air India privatisation

Each passing week unfolded a new sub-plot in the long drawn out case of Air India privatisation. UK's Cairn Energy Plc brought a lawsuit on 14 May 2021 in US District Court for the Southern District of New York, that potentially can lead to seizing of Air India's overseas assets such as airplanes to recover USD 1.72 billion from the Indian government which an international arbitration tribunal had awarded after overturning levy of retrospective taxes.[16]

Reuters reported on 8 July 2021 that a Paris court had accepted Cairn Energy petition that Indian state-owned assets – some 20 centrally located properties in the city worth – 20 million euros ($24 million) be frozen.[17] *Business Standard* in its editorial comment on 8 July 2021, 'Humilating seizure', said that the government's arrogance and inefficiency have led to this embarrassing situation. Arrogance, because it has failed to understand that treaties freely entered into cannot simply be ignored; and inefficiency, because it has failed to pursue its legal options effectively and also was unable to foresee the consequences of a loss. Beyond the monetary loss is the hit to India's status as an investment destination.[18]

Another company, Devas Multimedia Pvt., which was seeking over $1.2 billion it won in international arbitration from India, also filed a petition in New York asking Air India to pay the amount or forfeit its US property including planes, cargo handling equipment, and artwork.[19]

To take care of the root cause behind these cases, the government introduced the Taxation Laws (Amendment) Bill 2021 on 5 August 2021 to do away with the contentious retrospective tax law of 2012, which was used to raise tax demands on foreign investors like Vodafone and Cairn Energy. The Parliament passed the Bill on 9 August 2021.[20]

The last date for making financial bids for Air India was kept as 15 September 2021. It was reported that the Transaction Advisor received multiple bids which included Tata group and the SpiceJet Ajay Singh-led Consortium.

Tata Sons win Air India bid

In early October 2021, the government announced that the Air India Specific Alternative Mechanism (a group of ministers headed by union home minister) approved the highest price bid of M/s Talace Pvt Ltd, a wholly owned subsidiary of Tata Sons for sale of 100% equity share-holding of Government of India in Air India and Air India Express Limited, and 50% stake in ground handling firm Air India SATS. The winning bid of Tata Sons was ₹ 18,000 crore, of which ₹15,300 crore was debt and balance ₹ 2,700 crore in cash. To make the deal more palatable to the new owners, the government took the bulk of the airline's debt, to the extent of ₹ 46,000 crore. The second contestant in the bid process was the consortium led by SpiceJet Chairman Ajay Singh whose bid was of ₹ 15,100 crore, of which ₹ 12,835 crore was taking debt and ₹ 2,265 crore in cash. The reserve enterprise price as fixed by the government was ₹ 12,906 crore.

Tatas would additionally pay around ₹ 9,185 crore on lease obligations of 42 leased aircrafts. The transaction does not include non-core assets like land and buildings valued at ₹ 14,718 crore which would be transferred to Government of India 's Air India Asset Holding Limited (AIAHL), a special purpose vehicle. However, the buyer can use three buildings of Air India – The Air India building at Nariman Point, Mumbai; The Airlines House, New Delhi; and one training centre; for a period of two years. Also, apartments of Air India can be occupied for a period of six months.

The acquisition will give Tata some 120 planes, mostly older narrow body Airbus aircraft but also some newer wide body Boeing planes. It will get an additional 4,400 domestic and 1,800 international slots at Indian airports annually, as well as 900 slots at airports overseas, the most lucrative of which are at London's Heathrow. Tata will gain 8,000 full-time employees, which it must retain for at least one year under the terms of the deal, and if any of them is laid off after this period, the company must offer them a voluntary retirement scheme (VRS).

It is expected that the transaction between the Government and Tata Sons would be finalised by the end of December 2021. With the completion of the deal, Air India would be back in the hands of the group which founded it as Tata Airlines in 1932 before it was nationalised in 1953. The Tata Sons emeritus chairman Ratan Tata tweeted on 8 October 2021, that while it will take considerable effort to rebuild Air India's reputation, it would provide Tata with a strong opportunity in the aviation industry. 'Welcome back, Air India!' he said in a tweet.[21-23]

There is euphoria and expectation for fast privatisations after the Modi government's first successful privatisation in seven years. However, the process of privatisation is long drawn out and complicated. At present the government is simultaneously pursing two tracks – monetisation and privatisation. One has to watch that there remains adequate appetite and capacity on the part of acquiring entities.

References

1. Eleventh Series, Vol. XIV No. 11, Thursday, May 15, 1997, Lok Sabha Debates (English Version) Fourth Session (Part IV) (Eleventh Lok Sabha), Lok Sabha Secretariat, Delhi), accessed 14 June 2021, https://eparlib.nic.in/bitstream/123456789/3236/1/lsd_11_4_15-05-1997.pdf
2. Disinvestment Commission Report V to VIII), August 1998, accessed 14 June 2021, https://mail.google.com/mail/u/0/?tab=rm#inbox/FMfcgzGkX mfdZGPTsDbgfdGXWvWpDrxD
3. Parliamentary Standing Committee Report on Transport & Tourism regarding Air India, 2000, accessed 15 June 2021, http://164.100.47.5/rs/book2/reports/t_and_t/44threport.htm
4. First Annual Report of the National Aviation Company of India Limited (NACIL) – Directors Report, accessed 15 June 2021, www.airindia.in/writereaddata/Portal/FinancialReport/1_114_1_Directors_report_0708.pdf
5. The Economic Times, 'Indian Airlines merger has caused Air India's downfall: Ashwani Lohani', 1 July 2016, accessed 14 June 2021, https://economictimes.indiatimes.com/opinion/interviews/indian-airlines-merger-has-caused-air-indias-downfall-ashwani-lohani/articleshow/52998986.cms
6. Parliamentary Committee on Public Undertakings, 'Review of loss making CPSUs', Twenty Fourth Report, 2018–19, accessed 26 May 2021. http://164.100.47.193/lsscommittee/Public%20Undertakings/16_Public_Undertakings_24.pdf
7. HeatherTimmons, 'Losses rise as pilots and passengers forsake state-owned Air India', *The New York Times*, 26 May 2011, print version.
8. PTI, 'Air India mops up Rs 724 crore via assets monetisation plan', *Mint*. 20 December 2018, accessed 26 May 2021, www.livemint.com/Home-Page/nBAHd0CYVbcZCsOAYtCc9O/Air-India-mops-up-Rs724-crore-via-assets-monetisation-plan.html
9. Committee on Public Undertakings (2018–19), 'Review of loss making CPSUs', Lok Sabha Secretariat, New Delhi, December 2018, accessed on 26 May 2021, http://164.100.47.193/lsscommittee/Public%20Undertakings/16_Public_Undertakings_24.pdf
10. Mihir Mishra, 'Government invites bids to sell 76 per cent stake in Air India', *The Economic Times*, 29 March 2018, https://economictimes.indiatimes.com/industry/transportation/airlines-/-aviation/government-calls-out-bids-to-sale-76-per-cent-stake-in-air-india/articleshow/63517638.cms?from=mdr

11. Firstpost, 'Joint ownership of Air India with govt difficult proposition: IndiGo founder Rakesh Gangwal', 6 July 2017, www.firstpost.com/business/joint-ownership-of-air-india-with-govt-difficult-proposition-indigo-founder-rakesh-gangwal-3784313.html

12. Ministry of Civil Aviation, 'Preliminary Information Memorandum (PIM) for strategic disinvestment of Air India issued', PIB, 27 January 2020, accessed 26 May 2021, https://pib.gov.in/PressReleasePage.aspx?PRID= 1600699

13. Pranav Mukul, 'Key change in Air India disinvestment: Bidders can decide debt burden level', *The Indian Express*, 30 October 2020, https://indianexpress.com/article/india/air-india-disinvestment-debt-burden-6909328/

14. The Economic Times, 'Air India must be privatised or it will close down: Hardeep Singh Puri', 15 September 2020, accessed 14 June 2021, https://economictimes.indiatimes.com/industry/transportation/airlines-/-aviation/air-india-must-be-privatised-or-it-will-close-down-hardeep-singh-puri/videoshow/78131595.cms?from=mdr

15. Arindam Majumdar, 'Govt likely to fetch around Rs 15,000 crore from sale of Air India', *Business Standard*, 4 February 2021, accessed 26 May 2021, www.business-standard.com/article/economy-policy/govt-likely-to-fetch-around-rs-15-000-crore-from-sale-of-air-india-121020400014_1.html

16. The Economic Times, 'Cairn Energy sues Air India in US court to enforce $1.2 billion arbitration award', 15 May 2021, accessed 26 May 2021, https://economictimes.indiatimes.com/industry/energy/oil-gas/cairn-energy-sues-air-india-to-enforce-1-2-bln-arbitration-award-court-filing/articleshow/82653353.cms?from=mdr

17. Aditi Shah and Aftab Ahmed, 'Cairn wins freeze on India state assets in Paris in bid to recover tax damages', *Reuters*, 8 July 2021, www.reuters.com/world/india/cairn-wins-freeze-indias-state-owned-assets-paris-recover-tax-award-2021-07-08/

18. Business Standard Editorial Comment, 'Humilating seizure', 8 July 2021. www.business-standard.com/article/opinion/humiliating-seizure-1210 70801502_1.html

19. Upmanyu Trivedi and Anurag Kotoky, 'Now Devas wants to seize Air India's assets in the US to enforce $1.2 bn arbitration award', *The Print*, 29 June 2021, https://theprint.in/economy/now-devas-wants-to-seize-air-indias-assets-in-the-us-to-enforce-1-2-bn-arbitration-award/686518/

20. The Hindu, 'Rajya Sabha returns bill to end all retrospective taxation', 9 August 2021, www.thehindu.com/news/national/rajya-sabha-returns-bill-to-end-all-retrospective-taxation/article35815622.ece

21. Reuters, 'Tata regains control of troubled Air India with $2.4 bln bid', Aftab Ahmed and Aditi Shah, 8 October 2021. www.reuters.com/world/india/tata-wins-bid-take-over-troubled-state-run-air-india-2021-10-08/

22. Business Standard, 'Tata Sons makes winning bid of Rs 18,000 cr for Air India: Govt'. www.business-standard.com/article/economy-policy/tata-sons-emerges-as-the-top-bidder-for-air-india-govt-121100800678_1.html

23. Business Standard, 'Air India returns to Tatas after group puts in winning bid of Rs 18,000 cr', Nikunj Ohri and Arindam Mujamdar, 9 October 2021, www.business-standard.com/article/companies/air-india-returns-to-tatas-after-group-puts-in-winning-bid-of-rs-18-000-cr-121100800762_1.html

8 Privatisation of Bharat Petroleum Corporation Limited (BPCL)

Evolution of BPCL

The Government of India nationalised three foreign oil companies under the Act on the Nationalisation of Foreign Oil companies – ESSO (1974), Burma Shell (1976), and Caltex (1977).

On 24 January 1976, the Burmah Shell was taken over by the Government of India to form Bharat Refineries Limited. On 1 August 1977, it was renamed Bharat Petroleum Corporation Limited. BPCL is a holding company which engages in refining of crude oil and marketing of petroleum products. It operates Mumbai Refinery, Kochi Refinery, Bina Refinery, and Numaligarh Refinery.

BPCL was given status of *Maharatna* (roughly translated as a great jewel) CPSE in September 2017.

Financials of BPCL

There are seven Indian companies in the Fortune 500 list (based on total revenues) for 2021. Three are private sector companies (Reliance, Rajesh Exports, Tata Motors), and four are CPSEs (State Bank of India, Indian Oil, ONGC, and BPCL).

Let's look at the financials of BPCL (Table 8.1).

Privatising BPCL: a Maharatna CPSE in the oil sector

On 20 November 2019, the Cabinet Committee on Economic Affairs, chaired by the Prime Minister, accorded 'in-principle' approval for strategic disinvestment of the Government of India's entire shareholding of 52.98% in Bharat Petroleum Corporation Ltd.[1]

Mukul Kumar, convenor, Federation of Oil PSU Officers (FOPO) and Confederation of Maharatna Companies (COMCO) claiming to

DOI: 10.4324/9781003262213-9

Table 8.1 BPCL – profit and loss from 2020–21 to 2016–17 (in crore of ₹)

S. No.	Details	Financial year				
		2020–21	2019–20	2018–19	2017–18	2016–17
	REVENUE					
1	Operating revenue	232,545	284,383	297,275	236,421	202,210
2	Other income	4,344	3,081	2,983	2,911	2,600
3	**Total revenue**	236,889	287,464	300,258	239,332	204,811
	EXPENSES					
4	**Total expenses incl. depreciation and amortisation**	220,721	283,712	289,819	228,046	193,768
5	**Profits before exceptional items**	16,168	3,751	10,439	11,286	11,042
6	**Exceptional items**	6,449	1,080	-	-	-
7	**Profit before tax**	22,617	2,671	10,439	11,286	11,042
8	**Total tax expense**	3,576	(-) 12	3,307	3,309	3,003
9	**Profit after tax**	19,041	2,683	7,132	7,976	8,039

Source: Created by author based on money control, Bharat Petroleum Corporation Ltd, Financials, www.moneycontrol.com/financials/bharatpetroleumcorporation/profit-lossVI/BPC

represent over 70,000 officers of the top state owned firms, at a press conference on 8 December 2019, said that the government was killing the goose that lays golden eggs by privatising the highly profitable BPCL to meet the government's fiscal deficit target. He added that BPCL a Maharatna company and part of the Fortune 500 list of companies for 15 years, pays more than ₹17,000 crore as dividend to the central government. It has 6,000 acres of land across India, of which 750 acres is in Mumbai alone.[2]

The oil sector has been considered a strategic sector and privatising a profitable CPSE having a ranking in global Fortune 500 companies was a big decision taken by the government. This decision could have been possible because of the overwhelming majority the ruling party BJP had in 2019 election. Privatising a Maharatna CPSE in oil sector was a politically sensitive issue.

While participating in a discussion in December 2019 on 'Should the government exit Navratna companies?', C. P. Chandrasekhar, Centre of Economics Studies and Planning, Jawaharlal Nehru University, opined that earlier understanding was that you go in for partial disinvestment to public sector equity with two purposes, among many. One was it would allow you to mobilise a certain amount of resources which can be put into some kind of a fund which could be used to modernise, renovate, or make viable public sector firms which still have the possibility of being profitable despite being loss-making. In case of closure of an enterprise, this money could also be used to pay off workers and clean the books. The other purpose was that the private equity holding in public firms brings in a certain degree of monitoring and discipline of managers. We have clearly shifted from both of these, he said.[3]

Earlier, plans to privatise HPCL and BPCL in February 2002 during the government headed by Atal Bihari Vajpayee were thwarted by the Supreme Court. While hearing the Centre for Public Interest Litigation (CPIL) petition, the apex court held: 'There is no challenge before this Court (Supreme Court) as to the policy of disinvestment. The only question raised before us (is) whether the method adopted by the Government in exercising its executive powers to disinvest HPCL and BPCL without repealing or amending the law is permissible or not. We find that on the language of the Act such a course is not permissible at all,' Justice S. Rajendra Babu and G. P. Mathur stated in the 16 September 2003 order 'restraining the Central Government from proceeding with disinvestment resulting in HPCL and BPCL ceasing to be Government companies without appropriately amending the statutes concerned suitably.'[4]

In 2016, however, the Modi government did away with the legal roadblock by passing 'Repealing and Amending Act of 2016', which annulled 187 old laws including the Act of 1976 that had nationalised erstwhile Burmah Shell.[5]

Hindustan Petroleum Corporation Ltd (HPCL) was acquired by the Oil and Natural Gas Corporation (ONGC) on 1 February 2018, through an all cash deal worth ₹36,915 crore. ONGC financed the deal by taking ₹35,000 crore from seven banks including three private and four public sector banks to fund the acquisition.[6]

Strategic disinvestment of BPCL

On 20 November 2019, the Cabinet Committee on Economic Affairs, chaired by Prime Minister accorded 'in-principle' approval for strategic disinvestment of Government of India's entire shareholding of 52.98% in Bharat Petroleum Corporation Ltd (except its equity shareholding of 61.65% in Numaligarh Refinery Limited (NRL) and management control thereon) along with transfer of management control to a strategic buyer. Further, the Cabinet approved strategic disinvestment of BPCL's shareholding of 61.65% in NRL along with transfer of management control to a Central Public Sector Enterprise (CPSE) operating in the Oil and Gas Sector.[7]

A consortium of Oil India Ltd, Engineers India Ltd, and the Government of Assam expressed interest in buying the stake in NRL and the BPCL board approved the sale for ₹9,876 crore in March 2021.[8]

Invitation for expression of interest (EOI)

Having concluded the necessary step of selling its stake in Numaligarh Refinery Ltd which the government had announced would not be part of the disinvestment of BPCL, the government invited bids for the sale of its entire 52.98% stake in BPCL on 7 March 2020. The last date to submit EOI had to be extended multiple times and finally it closed on 16 November 2020. Important steps taken in-between this period were:

VRS. Ahead of the privatisation, BPCL decided to offer Voluntary Retirement to its employees which opened on 23 July and closed on 13 August 2020. Around 1,500 employees at BPCL went for the Voluntary Retirement Scheme (VRS).[9]

Increase in FDI. Earlier, FDI of 49% was permitted through automatic route in petroleum refining by the public sector undertakings (PSU), without any disinvestment or dilution of domestic equity in the existing PSUs. With this provision, a foreign player would not be able to buy more than 49% stake in BPCL. DIPAM suggested to amend the existing FDI policy to allow 100% foreign direct investment in a central public sector enterprise (CPSE) in the petroleum and natural gas sector.[10] In July 2021, the Government allowed 100% FDI in BPCL privatisation.[11]

Response to expression of interest (EOI)

It is reported that besides mining-to-oil conglomerate Vedanta who has put in an Expression of Interest, the other two are US-based private equity firms Apollo Global and I Squared Capital's arm Think Gas.[12]

It is understood that industry giants such as Reliance or even international big players like Aramco, Total, and BP have not participated in the bid. Another energy giant Russia's Rosneft-led Nayara Energy, which operates a 20 million tonne oil refinery in Vadinar in Gujarat, was expected as a potential bidder, but reports indicated that it was no longer keen to move ahead with it. None of the major international oil companies – who are actively seeking to enter the Indian energy market – showed interest either.[13]

Bloomberg reported that India has allowed bidders access to the financial data of Bharat Petroleum Corp. since the last week of April

2021. The government's 53% stake in the refiner was valued at about ₹50,900 crore ($6.9 billion) based on 7 May 2021 closing price.[14]

Life would come full circle for Bharat Petroleum Corporation Ltd. What started off as Burmah Shell, with foreign ownership – a joint venture of Royal Dutch, Shell and Rothschild, will again be a private company, but who would be the owner?

The BPCL privatisation is crucial for the government as it needs to raise resources to make up the fall in tax revenues as the pandemic hit the economy. However, the moot question remains that whether privatising BPCL for short-term gain to capture future earnings in one lump sum vis-a-vis steady future dividend income is prudent. The case of ENI in Italy which divested in 5 tranches, and the State still retains 30% in the cash rich company (dealt in Chapter 4)is instructive.

References

1. PIB, Cabinet Committee on Economic Affairs (CCEA), 'Cabinet approves strategic disinvestment of CPSEs', 20 November 2019, https://pib.gov.in/PressReleasePage.aspx?PRID=1592540
2. Business Standard, 'Plans to privatise BPCL suicidal for nation, says PSU Officers' Union', 9 December 2019, www.business-standard.com/article/pti-stories/officers-union-opposes-bpcl-privatisation-119120901162_1.html
3. T. T. Ram Mohan and C. P. Chandrasekhar, 'Should the government exit Navratna companies', *The Hindu*, 20 December 2019, www.thehindu.com/opinion/op-ed/should-the-government-exit-navratna-companies/article30351524.ece,
4. Centre For Public Interest vs Union Of India & Anr, Writ Petition (civil) 171 of 2003 With Writ Petition (Civil) No. 171 of 2003, and 286 of 2003, Judgement pronounced on 16 September 2003 by Supreme Court Bench of Justice S. Rajendra Babu and Justice G. P. Mathur, accessed 26 May 2021, https://indiankanoon.org/doc/1648759/
5. Apoorva Mandhani,The Print, 'How Modi govt quietly repealed old laws to pave the way for BPCL disinvestment', 25 November 2019, https://theprint.in/india/how-modi-govt-quietly-repealed-old-laws-to-pave-the-way-for-bpcl-disinvestment/325097/
6. ET Energy, 'ONGC completes Rs 36,915 crore HPCL acquisition, becomes first integrated oil major', 1 February 2018, https://energy.economictimes.indiatimes.com/news/oil-and-gas/ongc-completes-rs-36915-crore-hpcl-acquisition-becomes-first-integrated-oil-major/62725587
7. PIB, Cabinet Committee on Economic Affairs (CCEA), 'Cabinet approves strategic disinvestment of CPSEs', 20 November 2019, https://pib.gov.in/PressReleasePage.aspx?PRID=1592540

8. The Times of India, 'BPCL sells 54.16% stake in NRL to OIL; 4.4% to EIL', 27 March 2021,https://timesofindia.indiatimes.com/business/india-business/bpcl-sells-54-16-stake-in-nrl-to-oil-4-4-to-eil/articleshow/81714043.cms

9. ShreyaAmbre, 'Only 12% Bharat Petroleum employees opted for VRS; Privatization by March?', Trak.in, 24 August 2020, https://trak.in/tags/business/2020/08/24/only-12-bharat-petroleum-employees-opted-for-vrs-privatization-by-march/

10. Press Trust of India, 'Govt considering FDI policy tweak to facilitate privatisation of BPCL', *Business Standard*, 28 May 2021, www.businessstandard.com/article/economy-policy/govt-considering-fdi-policy-tweak-to-facilitate-privatisation-of-bpcl-121052800288_1.html

11. The Telegraph online,' Centre allows 100 percent FDI in BPCL privatisation', 23 July 2021, www.telegraphindia.com/business/centre-allows-100-fdi-in-bpcl-privatisation/cid/1823553

12. The Free Press Journal, 'Entry of big Pvt equity players set to heat up BPCL takeover', 17 December 2020, www.freepressjournal.in/business/entry-of-big-pvt-equity-players-set-to-heat-up-bpcl-takeover

13. Hiroo Advani and Kanika Arora, 'India: Privatisation of BPCL: Odds of it becoming a success story', Mondaq, 22 December 2020, accessed 26 May 2021, www.mondaq.com/india/oil-gas-electricity/1018632/privatisation-of-bpcl-odds-of-it-becoming-a-success-story

14. Baiju Kalesh and Debit Chakraborty,' Govt gives bidders data access for $7-billion Bharat Petroleum Sale', Bloomberg, 7 May 2021, accessed 26 May 2021, www.bloomberg.com/news/articles/2021-05-07/india-said-to-give-bidders-data-access-for-7-billion-bpcl-sale

9 Privatisation of airports

Introduction

The first airport privatisation took place in UK. British Airports Authority (BAA) was established by the Airport Authority Act 1965 and operated London Heathrow, Gatwick, Stansted, and four Scottish airports. BAA was privatised in 1987 as a single entity. The methodology used was offer for sale to general public, and institutions at fixed price, and a portion was sold by tender. It became a controversial issue until the UK Competition Commission concluded that common ownership gave rise to adverse effects on competition. BAA then divested Gatwick in 2009, Edinburgh in 2012, and Stansted in 2013.

Privatisation of airports has been undertaken by many countries though the scope and extent of privatisation has varied. Different types of privatisation models have been applied depending on the government's objectives, and the specific circumstances and requirements of the airport. Common objectives have been to provide new investment funds, improving quality of service, and performance. In the early stages of privatisation, investors were typically established airport operators or international infrastructure companies. Of late, investors are dominated by international funds from financial institutions, such as infrastructure funds, pension funds, insurance funds, and sovereign wealth funds.

Anne Graham (2020) wrote that a popular model in the early stages of privatisation was share flotation /initial public offering (IPO) / equity market issue by government. Airports which followed this model were BAA (1987), Vienna (1992), Copenhagen (1994), Zurich (2000), Fraport (2001), Paris (2005), Auckland (1998), Malaysia (1999), and Thailand (2004). However, this model was given up in favour of trade sale or very long lease to a single or more commonly a consortium of investors. Airports which followed this model were Dusseldorf (1998), Turin (2000), Rome (2000), Malta (2002), Milan (2011), Toulouse

DOI: 10.4324/9781003262213-10

(2015), Lyon (2016), South Africa (1998), Wellington (1998), Sydney (2002) [Anne Graham (2020), Para 2.1, first para].[1]

India adopted the public–private partnership (PPP) model and developed airports at Cochin (1999), Bangalore (2004), Hyderabad (2004), Delhi (2006), and Mumbai (2006). Currently, Adani Group holds 74% stake in Mumbai, and GMR Group holds 54% stake in Delhi and 63% stake in Hyderabad. Bangalore has 74% private promoters holding. In 2019, India privatised six airports at Ahmedabad, Lucknow, Jaipur, Mangaluru, Guwahati, and Thiruvananthapuram. The bids for all the six airports was won by Adani Group, a business conglomerate close to ruling party. Critics said that giving all the six airports to one entity adversely effects competition.

For the Financial Year 2021–22, the government proposes to privatise six airports in Tier 2/3 cities – Amritsar, Varanasi, Bhubaneswar, Indore, Raipur, and Trichy through brownfield PPP models. These six airports would be paired/clubbed with seven other smaller airports and leased out. It is to be seen how this round of privatisation is structured. The government has approved divestment of Airports Authority of India (AAI's) residual stake in the four airports at Mumbai, Delhi, Hyderabad, and Bangalore during FY 2022.

Airport operations in India

As on 31 March 2021, there are 125 operational airports under Airports Authority of India (AAI), a statutory body (created through the Airports Authority of India Act, 1994). AAI is under the Directorate General of Civil Aviation, Ministry of Civil Aviation, Government of India. Out of 125 airports, 29 are international, 86 domestic, and 10 are customs airports. Among 29 international airports, there are 3 civil enclaves, and 5 joint venture airports. Among 86 domestic airports, 20 are civil enclave operational airports, and 11 are State government/ private airports.[2]

Customs airports are notified by customs authorities for unloading of imported goods and loading of export goods. Civil enclave airports are generally civil enclaves that are part of airports of armed forces and are used for commercial flights.

Airports Authority of India (AAI)

The International Airports Authority of India (IAAI) was constituted as an autonomous body under the International Airports Authority Act of 1971. Four international airports – Delhi, Bombay, Madras, and

Calcutta – were transferred to the IAAI with effect from 1 April 1972. Later Trivandrum Airport was also transferred to IAAI.

In 1985, a similar need was felt for domestic airports and air traffic control and related services. Consequently, the National Airports Authority (NAA) was constituted under the National Airports Authority Act of 1985.

Eventually, IAAI and NAA were merged into what is now known as the Airports Authority of India (AAI). It is a statutory body created through the Airports Authority of India Act, 1994. AAI provides air traffic services to all arriving, departing, and en-route aircraft over Indian airspace. All airports in India were under control of AAI till 1999, before start of CIAL Cochin International Airport Limited (CIAL).[3]

Airports Economic Regulatory Authority (AERA) and Appellate Authority

Airports Economic Regulatory Authority (AERA) is a regulatory agency under Government of India to regulate tariffs and other charges for services rendered at major airports. It is a statutory body constituted under Airports Economic Regulatory Authority of India Act (AERA) 2008. 'Major airport' meant any airport that has, or is designated to have, annual passenger traffic in excess of 1.5 million. This definition of 'major airport' was amended in August 2019, as one in excess of annual passenger traffic 35 lakh (3.5 million).[3]

The 2019 amendment act also included that AERA will not determine the tariff or tariff structures or the amount of development fees in respect of an airport or part thereof, if such tariff or tariff structures or the amount of development fees has been incorporated in the bidding document that awards operatorship of that airport. This amendment is of far reaching consequences. There was however a proviso that the Authority shall be consulted in advance regarding the tariff, tariff structures or the amount of development fees proposed to be incorporated in the bidding document.[3]

In 2021, the Airports Economic Regulatory Authority of India (Amendment) Bill was passed which allowed tariff determination of a 'group of airports' by way of amending the definition of 'major airport'. The Bill adds that the central government may group airports and notify the group as a major airport.[4] This amendment would facilitate pairing of smaller, non-profitable airports with profitable airports as a package to bidders to make it a viable combination for investment under PPP mode. The amendment bill became an Act on 12 August 2021.

The Airports Economic Regulatory Authority Appellate Tribunal was established to adjudicate disputes and dispose of appeals in 2010. As per the Finance Act of 2017, the Airports Economic Regulatory Authority Appellate Tribunal and the Cyber Appellate Tribunal (established under the Information Technology Act of 2000) have been merged with the Telecom Disputes Settlement and Appellate Tribunal (TDSAT). As such, TDSAT exercises original as well as appellate jurisdiction in regard to airport tariff matters.[5]

Privatisation of airports in India

Cochin International Airport Ltd (CIAL) was the first Indian airport to be constructed and operated in public–private partnership (PPP) model and started operations in 1999. Such was the interest in this PPP model that Kennedy School of Government, Harvard University; and National University of Singapore jointly wrote a case in 2001, 'Cochin International Airport: The Gateway to God's Own Country'. The shareholders of CIAL are the Government of Kerala, financial institutions, and around 18,000 shareholders from more than 25 countries,[6]

The Government of India handed over four major airports – Bangalore, Delhi, Hyderabad, and Mumbai to private companies under PPP agreement. In 2019, six airports at Ahmedabad, Lucknow, Jaipur, Mangaluru, Guwahati, and Thiruvananthapuram were privatised. In 2020, the Government approved privatisation of another six airports by bundling them with seven smaller airports to be done in FY 2021–22.

The upcoming NOIDA International Airport at Jewar on the outskirts of Delhi is also to be developed by a private company. Zurich Airport International was given the licence in October 2020 to design, build, and operate Noida International Airport (NIAL) for the next 40 years. *Business Standard* (17 July 2021) reported that the agreement has been signed with NIAL.[7] The PM laid foundation stone of the airport on 25 November 2021.

Mumbai International Airport Ltd (MIAL)

GVK Group, a leading Indian conglomerate, began its foray in airports 2006 as it won the bid to manage Mumbai Airport. However, GVK's inability to meet its debt liabilities and pressure from borrowers forced it to sell its stake to Gautam Adani-led Adani group in September 2020. *Business Standard* (1 September 2020) reported that under the transaction, Adani Airport Holdings (AAHL), the holding company of Adani Group for its airports business, acquired a 50.5% stake in the GVK

group. Additionally, AAHL also acquired 23.5% of minority partners –
Airport Company of South Africa (ACSA) and Bidvest. ACSA and
Bidvest held 10% and 13.5% stake respectively in MIAL. Adani group
thus acquired 74% stake in MIAL . Having acquired 74% in MIAL
gives Adanis control of Navi Mumbai Airport, the upcoming second
airport in Mumbai in which MIAL holds a 74% stake.[8]

The deal between GVK and Adani Groups marked the culmination
of a two-year-long fight during which the Reddy family – owner of the
GVK group – scouted for buyers, struck binding agreements with a consortium of foreign investors, and fought legal battles to thwart the Adani
group's hostile takeover attempts. In the end, the Reddys succumbed to
the default pressure from the lenders' consortium, led by State Bank of
India. Losing control of Mumbai Airport follows GVK group's earlier
exit from the Bengaluru Airport in 2017. This probably meant an end to
the firm's airport business which began in 2006 with Mumbai Airport.[8]

Delhi International Airport Ltd (DIAL), and Hyderabad International Airport

After privatisation in 2006, GMR Group holding in DIAL was 54%.
AAI held 26%, Fraport AG 10%, and Eraman Malaysia 10%. The
GMR holding in Hyderabad International Airport was 63% and AAI
along with the Government of Andhra Pradesh held 26%.

In February 2020, the GMR Infrastructure Ltd, the company
that operates Delhi and Hyderabad airports, signed a share purchase
agreement to sell 49% stake in its airports' business to France's Groupe
Airport De Paris (ADP). *Business Standard* (8 July 2020) reported that
the deal was restructured due to Covid-19's impact on aviation industry,
and the French airport operator paid ₹ 9,720 crore instead of ₹ 10,780
crore earlier agreed to. GMR Infrastructure and Groupe ADP would
now be the majority shareholders operating Delhi and Hyderabad
Airports.[9]

Bangalore International Airport Ltd (BIAL)

Bangalore International Airport Limited (BIAL), renamed as
Kempegowda International Airport, Bengaluru, was incorporated in
January 2001. BIAL under a concession agreement with the Government
of India until the year 2038 (with the right to extend the agreement for
an additional 30 years) has the exclusive rights to carry out the development, design, financing, construction, commissioning, maintenance,
operation, and management of the airport through a public–private

partnership. It claimed to be the first greenfield airport in India built through a public–private partnership.

It started operations in May 2008. Private promoters hold 74% in BIAL. After buying 6% of Siemens holding in 2018, Fairfax India Holdings (part of Canada's Fairfax Financial Holdings) has 54%, and Siemens Projects Ventures 20%. The balance is held by Karnataka State Industrial & Infrastructure Development Corporation Limited, Government of Karnataka (13%); and Airports Authority of India, Government of India (13%).[10]

In March 2021, Fairfax India Holdings filed for listing in stock exchange, 'Anchorage Infrastructure Investment Holdings Ltd' (a wholly owned unit of Fairfax India Holdings) to become its flagship company to invest in India's airport sector and for airport privatisation projects. The listing of Anchorage was to allow Fairfax to monetise its investment in Bangalore International Airport Ltd (BIAL), which operates the Kempegowda International Airport in Bengaluru city.[11]

Government to sell its residual stake in Delhi, Mumbai, Bangalore, and Hyderabad airports

The Government announced in 2021 that it has decided to sell its residual stake in already privatised Delhi, Mumbai, Bangalore (now Bengaluru) and Hyderabad airports as part of its ambitious asset monetisation plan. While AAI holding in Mumbai International Airport and Delhi International Airport is 26%, its holding along with the Government of Andhra Pradesh in Hyderabad International Airport Ltd is 26%, and a similar stake in Bangalore International Airport along with the Karnataka Government.[12]

Analysis of privatisation of airports in 2019 and 2020

The government announced in November 2018 that encouraged by its experience of managing five airports in Delhi, Mumbai, Bengaluru, Kochi, and Hyderabad through private participation, the union cabinet has approved a similar method in managing six more airports: Lucknow, Ahmedabad, Jaipur, Mangaluru, Thiruvananthapuram, and Guwahatifor operation, management and development (OMD) under public–private partnership (PPP).[13]

In February 2019, Adani Group emerged as the highest bidder for running all the six AAI airports on a 50-year lease. Adani Group had quoted highest per passenger fee (PPF) which was the bidding parameter. According to AAI, Adanis offered ₹177, ₹174, ₹171, ₹168, ₹115, and ₹160 per passenger for Ahmedabad, Jaipur, Lucknow, Thiruvananthapuram, Mangaluru, and Guwahati airports, respectively.[14]

Concession agreements for Ahmedabad, Lucknow, and Mangaluru airports were signed on 14 February 2020. The Adani group wrote to the Airport Authority of India (AAI) to invoke the force majeure clause, due to the coronavirus pandemic and delay taking over the three airports for at least six months.[15] Concession agreements for operating the other three airports, Jaipur, Guwahati, and Thiruvananthapuram, were signed on 19 January 2021 for 50 years lease.[16]

Awarding all six airports to Adani Enterprise: Controversy

The Adani group had acquired Mumbai airport (MIAL) from GVK group in September 2020, and now the six airports in year 2020 and 2021.

The *Financial Times* carried a story, ' "Modi's Rockefeller": Gautam Adani and the concentration of power in India' (13 November 2020).[17] It said that when the Indian government approved the privatisation of six airports in 2018, it relaxed the rules to widen the pool of competition, allowing companies without any experience in the sector to bid. There was one clear winner from the rule change: Gautam Adani, the billionaire industrialist with no history of running airports, scooped up all six.

It further added that Adani is India's largest private ports operator and thermal coal power producer. He commands a growing share of India's power transmission and gas distribution markets. 'Gautam Adani is very powerful, very politically well connected and very astute at using that power,' says Tim Buckley, an energy analyst based in Australia who tracks India. 'He is Modi's Rockefeller.' Adani continues to enjoy ample access to capital, both at home and overseas, and can tell investors that he has never defaulted on a loan despite highly leveraged balance sheets. 'He's become one of the most powerful men in India in the space of 20 years,' Buckley says. 'What he touches turns to gold.'

After more than two months of the criticism, the government issued a press note on 21 January 2021 stating that the bidding process was conducted in a competitive and transparent manner through e-tendering portal. The tender process of each airport was undertaken on individual basis. It clarified that the bid parameter stipulated in the tender document was 'per passenger fee' quoted by the bidder and the entity whose bid is highest in terms of per passenger fee quoted would be declared as successful bidder. The quote of M/s Adani Enterprises Limited was highest in all the six airports.[18]

Further, the government added that the terms and conditions of the transaction of the PPP were deliberated and decided on 17 November 2018 by the Empowered Group of Secretaries (EGOS), chaired by CEO NITI Aayog with Secretaries of Ministry/Department of Economic Affairs, Expenditure, and Civil Aviation. The government Press Note further said that the EGOS decision was agreed by Public Private Partnership Appraisal Committee (PPPAC) (another group of Secretaries) in its meeting on 11 December 2018.

It added that EGOS took a conscious decision not to put any restrictions on the number of airports to be bid for or to be awarded to a single entity considering the fact that these six airports are smaller in size and handling only 9.5% of the passenger traffic whereas Delhi and Mumbai airports accounted for more than 45% of the total passenger traffic in 2006 when they were brought under PPP and the decision to cap one airport to single bidder was necessary.

The government asserted that the quantum of passengers handled by the private airport operators is crucial and important than the number of airports handled by a single entity. Further, EGOS decided not to stipulate prior airport experience as a mandatory qualification to increase competition and avoid monopoly by those players having airport experience, who would have an edge over others.

Adani Enterprises now manages seven operational airports. The other major private players in the sector are GMR Group (which manages the Delhi, Hyderabad, and under-construction Mopa-Goa airports), Zurich Airport (developing the Jewar airport near Noida), and Fairfax (Bengaluru airport).

Proposed monetisation of airports in 2021–22

In March 2021, the Government decided to privatise 13 airports, currently under the Airports Authority of India, packaged in six buckets with a mix of a profitable and an under-performing airport to be monetised through the Operation, Management, and Development Agreement (OMDA) model.[19]

According to sources, the first bundle includes a combination of Tiruchi and Salem airports. By the end of FY20, Tiruchi earned a profit of ₹22.85 crore whereas Salem airport had incurred a loss of close to ₹8.76 crore.

The second basket includes Bhubaneswar and Jharsguda airports that have made, respectively, a profit of ₹34.22 crore and a loss of ₹16.29 crore.

The third bucket is of two airports in Madhya Pradesh – Indore and Jabalpur. Indore's airport made a profit of ₹4 crore in 2019–20 whereas Jabalpur incurred a loss of ₹19.24 crore the same fiscal year.

Raipur Airport and Jalgaon airports would be clubbed and both these airports incurred losses in FY20 – the Chhattisgarh capital of ₹26.75 crore and the latter of ₹3.72 crore.

Another pairing is of the Amritsar and Kangra airports. Amritsar's airport posted a profit of close to ₹92 lakh whereas Kangra, also known as Gaggal airport, posted a net loss of ₹9 crore.

The last bucket has three airports. It includes Varanasi, which posted a net loss of ₹ 1.6 crore; Gaya, which posted a net loss of ₹26 crore, and Kushinagar for which no data was available in public domain.

National Monetisation Pipeline announced in August 2021 that 25 major AAI airports are considered for monetisation over four years – 2021–22 to 2024–25. During 2021–22, AAI has identified six airports in Tier 2/ Tier 3 cities, namely Amritsar, Varanasi, Bhubaneswar, Indore, Raipur, and Trichy for the purpose of monetisation through brownfield PPP models. To ensure commensurate development of non-profitable airports along with the profitable airports with the help of private sector investment and participation, pairing/clubbing of smaller airports with each of the six bigger airports and leasing out as a package is being explored.[20]

Further, divestment of AAI's residual stake in four airport JVs has also been considered under the monetisation pipeline. This includes the private sector operated airports in Mumbai (26% stake), Delhi (26% stake), Hyderabad (13% stake), and Bangalore (13% stake).[20]

Bundling of airports in groups where some are profitable and some are not is in line with international experience (e.g. Mexico). The profits from the profitable airports can cross-subsidise the loss-making small airports which on their own may appear unattractive for privatisation.

Impact of Covid pandemic on airport privatisation

Until the end of 2019, the outlook for airport privatisation deals was looking positive with relatively strong traffic growth being forecast, and a growing need for capital investment in the industry. However, all this dramatically changed with the corona virus pandemic. It caused a severe unprecedented impact on the air transport industry with airport revenues falling sharply. Airport investment was no longer low risk which was capable of producing steady returns with proven longevity. The Association of Private Airport Operators appealed to the Government for urgent relief on 9 June 2021, as they were not generating sufficient cash flows to sustain operations and meet debt obligations.

While we discussed the privatisation of state owned Air India in Chapter 7, the aviation companies in private sector, Indigo, commanding half the domestic aviation market share, posted its fifth consecutive quarterly loss in Q 4 of 2020−21 of over ₹1,100 crore. One of the fastest-growing pre-pandemic airlines, Spicejet completely eroded its net worth. The Go Air (rechristened Go First) hit the market to raise funds to sustain the airline, while Tata-backed Vistara has deep pockets to dig into.[21]

References

1. Anne Graham, 'Airport privatisation: A successful journey?', *Journal Of Air Transport Mangement*, Elsevier (para 2.1). Published online. 19 Sep. 2020. doi: 10.1016/j.jairtraman.2020.101930 . (Free PMC article, Elsevier Public Health Emergency Collection, www.ncbi.nlm.nih.gov/pmc/articles/PMC7502006/)
2. Ministry of Civil Aviation, www.civilaviation.gov.in
3. Amir Singh Pasrich and Kshitij Paliwal, 'In brief: airport operations in India', Lexology, 14 August 2020, www.lexology.com/library/detail. aspx?g=3e40dbec-780f-4719-8970-be57fb56ff4e
4. Press Information Bureau, Government of India, Press Release, Ministry of Civil Aviation, 'Airports Economic Regulatory Authority of India Bill 2021 passed in Parliament', 4 August 2021. https://pib.gov.in/PressReleaseDetail. aspx?PRID=1742540
5. Amir Singh Pasrich and Kshitij Paliwal, 'In brief: airport operations in India', Lexology, 14 August 2020, www.lexology.com/library/detail. aspx?g=3e40dbec-780f-4719-8970-be57fb56ff4e
6. CIAL, https://cial.aero/contents/viewcontent.aspx?linkIdLvl2=51&link Id=51
7. Business Standard, PTI. 'Zurich Airport signs agreement with NIAL for development of Noida Airport', 17 July 2021, www.business-standard. com/article/economy-policy/zurich-airport-signs-agreement-with-nial-for-development-of-noida-airport-121071700462_1.html
8. Arindam Majumder, 'Adani Group acquires 74 per cent stake in Mumbai International Airport', *Business Standard*, 1 September 2020, www.business-standard.com/article/companies/adani-group-acquires-74-per-cent-stake-in-mumbai-international-airport-120083100215_1.html
9. ArindamMajumder, 'GMR restructure airport deal due to coronavirus pandemic', *Business Standard*, 8 July 2020, www.business-standard.com/article/companies/groupe-adp-gmr-restructure-airport-deal-due-to-coronavirus-pandemic-120070701813_1.html
10. BIAL, www.bengaluruairport.com/corporate/about-bial.html
11. Fairfax India Holdings Corporation News Release, 29 March 2018, https://s1.q4cdn.com/293822657/files/doc_news/2018/March/FIH-March-29-BIAL.pdf

12. The Telegraph online, 'Govt plans to sell residual stakes in Delhi, Mumbai, Bangalore and Hyderabad airports', 15 March 2021, www.telegraphindia. com/business/govt-plans-to-sell-residual-stakes-in-delhi-mumbai-bangalore-and-hyderabad-airports/cid/1809559

13. Prashant K. Nanda, Jyotika Sood, and Girish Chandra Prasad, 'Cabinet gives nod to private management of six more airports', *Mint*, 8 November 2018, www.livemint.com/Politics/qeENtSrB5sjdjOpVu237kN/Cabinet-gives-nod-to-private-management-of-six-more-airports.html

14. Arindam Majumdar, 'Govt likely to drop proposals to cap bids for airport privatisation', *Business Standard*, 12 December 2020. www. business-standard.com/article/economy-policy/govt-likely-to-drop-proposals-to-cap-bids-for-airport-privatisation-120121200035_1.html

15. Arindam Majumdar, 'Adani group seeks more time to take over 3 airports, cites coronavirus', *Business Standard*, 4 June 2020, www.business-standard. com/article/companies/adani-group-says-can-t-take-over-3-airports-cites-coronavirus-impact-120060400171_1.html

16. The New India Express, 20 January 2021,'Adani to get Guwahati, Thiruvananthapuram and Jaipur airports', www.newindianexpress. com/business/2021/jan/20/adani-to-get-guwahati-thiruvananthapuram-andjaipur-airports-2252513.html

17. Stephanie Findlay and Hudson Lockett, ' "Modi's Rockefeller": Gautam Adani and the concentration of power in India', *Financial Times*, 13 November 2020, www.ft.com/content/474706d6-1243-4f1e-b365-891d4c5d528b

18. Press Information Bureau, Government of India, Press Note, 21 January 2021, https://pib.gov.in/PressReleseDetailm.aspx?PRID=1690891

19. Forum Gandhi, '13 airports set for divestment packaged into six bundles', BusinessLine, 16 March 2021. www.thehindubusinessline.com/economy/logistics/13-airports-set-for-divestment-packaged-into-six-bundles/article34085523.ece

20. NITI Aayog, National Monetisation Pipeline, Volume II: Asset Pipeline, p. 76 www.niti.gov.in/sites/default/files/2021-08/Vol_2_NATIONAL_MONETISATION_PIPELINE_23_Aug_2021.pdf

21. Sai Manish, 'How Indian aviation sector braved Covid turbulence better than global peers', *Business Standard*, 11 June 2021, www.business-standard.com/article/companies/how-indian-aviation-sector-braved-covid-turbulence-better-than-global-peers-121061101398_1.html

10 Privatisation of banks

Why banks are special institutions

Banks are unique institutions in that they are depositories of public funds which they effectively hold as trusts. A huge amount of trust is placed in banks as repositories of people's money. Since banks intermediate these funds through credit creation, they are vulnerable to both credit risk and liquidity risk due to maturity and liquidity transformation. Banks form the bedrock of the payment system which lubricates the whole economy. Rakesh Mohan, a former Deputy Governor in Reserve Bank of India, wrote in *Business Standard* that bank failures involve externalities: they can lead to bank runs on other healthy banks and impose costs on bank borrowers. As banks have access to central bank money, the banks themselves and their owners have to be scrutinised carefully on a continuous basis and controlled (*Business Standard*, 14 December 2020).[1]

Nationalisation of banks in July 1969

The insurance sector was nationalised in 1956 with the formation of Life Insurance Corporation of India, but banks privatisation had to wait till 1969, barring the case of Imperial Bank already nationalised and renamed as State Bank of India in 1955.The Congress government felt that the private banks failed to support its socio-economic objectives of giving credit to agriculture sector, the share of which remained unchanged from 2% since 1951 to 1967. The share of industry in credit however increased from 34% in 1951 to 64.3% in 1967. As the private banks were run by big industrialists, it was alleged that they gave loans to themselves.[2]

On 19 July 1969, Indira Gandhi the Prime Minister and Finance Minister at that time announced a far-reaching decision of the

DOI: 10.4324/9781003262213-11

Government to nationalise 14 major Indian commercial banks. Threshold level for nationalisation was kept as ₹50 crore in deposits. Foreign banks were excluded.[i,3] About seven months later the Supreme Court of India invalidated the ordinance, but the Government used another Presidential ordinance to re-nationalise the banks.[4]

This decision of the Government brought about 80% of banking assets under the control of the state. The third volume of Reserve Bank of India's history stated that nationalisation of banks was the 'single most important economic decision taken by any government since 1947. Not even the reforms of 1991 are comparable in their consequences – political, social, and, of course, economic.'[5]

The story behind the hurry to bring bank nationalisation on 19 July 1969

The Congress Parliamentary Board met on 11 July 1969, to discuss the party's candidate for the forthcoming presidential election which was necessitated midway due to demise of President Zakir Hussain. The dominant group in the party called 'syndicate' had already decided on nominating Neelam Sanjeeva Reddy, the Speaker of Lok Sabha. The prime minister was forced to accept proposing Neelam Sanjeeva Reddy as the party candidate when he filed his nomination papers.[6] V. V. Giri, the Vice President of India who was the Acting President, announced his candidature as an independent candidate in the forthcoming presidential election.

Well known economist and politician Jairam Ramesh's biography of P. N. Haksar, 'Intertwined Lives: PN Haksar and Indira Gandhi', narrates the eventful days of July 1969.[7]

On 16 July the Prime Minister took the finance portfolio from Morarji Desai, who was also the deputy prime minister and close to the syndicate. Desai resigned from the cabinet. The same day, she asked P. N. Haksar, her closest aide, to meet K. N. Raj, one of India's most distinguished economists, and found out his views on bank nationalisation. Another eminent economist, P. N. Dhar, was also present when Haksar and Raj met. Dhar was to later write that Raj strongly favoured nationalisation but felt it would take at least six months to carry it out. But just three days later, on 19 July 1969, 14 banks were indeed nationalised.

The following narrative is from the memoirs of D. N. Ghosh, who was then the official concerned in the banking division of the Ministry of Finance and later became chairman of the State Bank of India (SBI).

It was the night of 17 July 1969 and Ghosh recalls being summoned to Haksar's residence, where he saw Haksar browsing through a mass of papers. He was trying to figure out how many banks accounted for 80–85% of the total resources of the system. Off the cuff, he said the number could be 10–12 banks. Bakshi deputy governor of the RBI also joined the duo late that night of 17 July 1969. For the next few hours, Haksar, Bakshi, Ghosh, and a few others who had been specially commandeered for this purpose, like R. K. Seshadri (an RBI official) and Niren De (attorney general) slogged to prepare the Ordinance.[8]

Ghosh also recounted that some four years after bank nationalisation, he and Haksar were travelling by train to Calcutta and he asked him whether he believed the decision taken in July 1969 with such great speed and secrecy was the right one. Haksar replied promptly: 'Of course, I have always believed so. We would have in any case taken that step, sooner or later. Timing was dictated by political necessity.'[9]

The Prime Minister addressed the nation on All India Radio and announced the nationalisation of banks on 19 July 1969. Bank Nationalisation Legislation was the last official order Giri signed as acting president before he stepped down on 20 July to enter the fray.

India's banking sector and agricultural credit

One of the reason for nationalisation of banks in July 1969, was agricultural credit share of total credit was too low. For a country like India, agricultural credit is important. Now, there is huge improvement. The Government of India (GoI) fixes the agricultural credit target every year for commercial banks, regional rural banks (RRBs), and rural co-operative banks.

During 2019–20, against the target of ₹13.5 lakh crore, banks have achieved ₹13.7 lakh crore (101.8% of the target), of which commercial banks, RRBs and rural co-operative banks achieved 109.2%, 73.9% and 92.8% of their respective targets. Further, the Kisan Credit Card (KCC) provided adequate and timely bank credit to farmers under a single window.[10] The agricultural credit target is ₹ 15 lakh crore for 2020–21, and ₹16.5 lakh crores for 2021–22.

India's financial sector is teeming with state-owned banks and insurance companies. Of the country's $2.52 trillion of bank assets, public sector banks (PSBs) control about $ 1.52 trillion, or 60%. PSBs typically have more than 75% government ownership.[11]

The key problem facing the financial sector at present is the lack of credit growth in view of the legacy overhang of large nonperforming assets, which is likely to get worse as a consequence of the ongoing

Covid crisis. The proposal in the Union government budget for the fiscal 2022 to promote bad bank (or by a consortium of banks) may help existing banks to be freed of the overhang.

Privatisation of banks – a strategic sector

The Union Finance Minister Nirmala Sitharaman, while presenting Union Government Budget 2021–22, announced that other than IDBI Bank, we propose to take up the privatisation of two public sector banks and one general insurance company in the year 2021–22. She also announced the Government's decision to amend the Insurance Act, 1938 to increase the permissible FDI limit from 49% to 74% in Insurance Companies and allow foreign ownership and control with safeguards. The FM stated that in 2021–22 we would bring the IPO of LIC.

The FM announced that National Asset Reconstruction Company Limited (NARCL), and Asset Management Company would be set up to consolidate and take over the existing stressed debt of public sector banks and then manage and dispose of the assets to alternate investment funds and other potential investors for eventual value realisation. To consolidate the financial capacity of PSBs, further recapitalisation of ₹ 20,000 crores was proposed during 2021–22.[12]

In mid-September 2021, the union government announced that the NARCL will acquire about ₹2 trillion in phases, and these sourced loans would be transferred by paying 15% cash to lenders and the remaining 85% would be paid through security receipts. These security receipts issued by the NARCL would be backed by a government guarantee of up to ₹30,600 crore. This guarantee will be valid for five years and will be tradable. A government guarantee can be invoked to cover the shortfall between the amount realised from the underlying assets and the face value of the security receipts issued for such assets, subject to an overall ceiling of ₹30,600 crore (*Business Standard*, 17 September 2021, p. 1).[13]

Ila Patnaik, a professor at the National Institute of Public Policy and Finance and former government adviser, said the plans sent 'a very important political signal'. 'For so many years, bank privatisation was off the cards,' she said. 'The fact that it has been announced – even before you have a plan of which banks – is a very strong pro-reformist, pro-market signal.' Rathin Roy, managing director of ODI London, a think-tank, said 'It's a good statement of intention, but there is nobody that I can see in the government that cares enough about privatisation and has the political capital to make this work.'[14]

The current privatisation plan of banks is an extension of the government's broader agenda to reform the Indian banking sector and reduce the number of state-owned banks further, which have come down from 27 in 2017 to 12 in 2020 after three successive rounds of consolidation.

Should large corporate houses be promoters of banks?

The Reserve Bank of India constituted an Internal Working Group (IWG) in June 2020 to review extant ownership guidelines and corporate structure for Indian private sector banks. The terms of reference of the IWG inter-alia included review of the eligibility criteria for individuals/entities to apply for a banking licence, and review of norms for long-term shareholding in banks by the promoters and other shareholders. The Report was made public on 28 November 28, 2020.

The IWG recommended the limit for promoter shareholdings to be raised from 15% to 26%, the non-promoter shareholdings limit be raised from 10% to 15% for all kinds of shareholders, including other industrial houses and presumably other banks. The IWG also recommended that banks can invest in other companies up to 20% of their paid up capital and reserves. If this is taken in conjunction with the proposal to allow large corporate/industrial houses to become bank promoters, it will enable the bank itself to then invest in the promoter's companies, once again bringing into question the separation of commercial and banking interests.[15]

Given the need to ensure appropriate and intrusive regulation and supervision of banks and their owners, the United States legislation mandates the designation of the owner of a bank holding company as a bank holding company itself, which implies that the regulator has full supervisory and inspection powers over the owner itself. A similar issue arises in India if the corporate/industrial house becomes the promoter of a bank through the bank holding company. The RBI would then need to extend consolidated supervision of the industrial house as a whole. Rakesh Mohan writes that this will not be feasible, both from the point of view of the industrial house and from that of the RBI. The industrial house would presumably not welcome such intrusive supervision, nor would the RBI have the regulatory or supervisory capacity to do so (*Business Standard*, 15 December 2020).[16]

IWG also recommended that well-run large Non-banking Financial Companies (NBFCs, with an asset size of ₹50,000 crore and above), including those which are owned by a corporate house, may be considered for conversion into banks provided they have completed 10 years of operations and meet the due diligence criteria.

Reasons for recommending corporate groups to own banks

The reason given for corporate houses to be promoter of banks is that India is under banked and it would bring much-needed new capital in the banking system. One of the arguments made is that the credit-GDP ratio in India is too low at around 50%, which is lower than in many other emerging markets, thereby providing evidence that India is under banked. Rakesh Mohan wrote in *Business Standard* that the correct way to assess whether India is under banked is to compare it with countries with similar per capita incomes. If a trend line is drawn of credit-GDP ratio with respect to per capita income, it is found that India has been above the trend line for at least the last 20 years. He buttresses his argument that based on the present data for over 160 countries, if India would be on the trend line, the credit-GDP ratio would need to be around 33% if the GDP per capita is taken at market exchange rates, and around 41% at purchasing power parity exchange rates. Thus, the credit-GDP ratio of around 50% can in no circumstances be seen as being too low. (*Business Standard*, 15 December 2020).[16]

Regarding the argument that corporate houses would bring the much-needed new capital in the banking system, it is suggested that it would be better if the private corporate/industrial groups use the capital they have to invest in economic activities that generate growth in output and employment, rather than their non-core activities.

Professor S. P. Kothari of MIT Sloan School of Management wrote in the *Economic Times*, that diffused ownership characterises most large US and British banks. For example, the three largest shareholders of JP Morgan Chase are the Vanguard Group (7.5%), State Street (4.4%) and Black Rock (4.1%). Their stakes are spread across several mutual funds (MFs) and exchange-traded funds (ETFs), none of them being an activist shareholder (Bank of America may be an exception, with Berkshire Hathaway's ownership of 11.7%). Absence of controlling stake of an owner family reduces the likelihood of the latter deriving private benefits at the expense of minority shareholders (*Economic Times*, 25 February 2021).[17]

An industrial house's ownership of a bank would result in conflicts of interest. It's therefore recommended to disallow industrial houses to gain controlling interest in a bank.

Regarding the two banks to be privatised, NITI Aayog, the government think tank, submitted the finalised names of PSU banks to the

Core Group of Secretaries on Disinvestment on 3 June 2021. Following the clearance from the Core Group of Secretaries, headed by the Cabinet Secretary, the finalised names will go to Alternative Mechanism (AM) for its approval and eventually to the Cabinet headed by the Prime Minister for the final nod.[18]

News channels reported on 21 June 2021 that the two shortlisted PSU banks to be privatised are Central Bank of India, and Indian Overseas Bank. The privatisation buzz lifted stocks of the two banks by 20%.[19]

Note

i Fourteen banks – Central Bank of India, Bank of India, Punjab National Bank, Bank of Baroda, United Commercial Bank, Canara Bank, United Bank of India, Dena Bank, Syndicate Bank, Union Bank of India, Allahabad Bank, Indian Bank, Bank of Maharashtra, and Indian Overseas Banks. A second round of nationalisations of six more commercial banks followed in 1980 (Punjab and Sind Bank, Vijaya Bank (later merged with Bank of Baroda), Oriental Bank of India (later merged with Punjab National Bank), Corporation Bank (later merged with Union Bank of India), Andhra Bank (later merged with Union Bank of India), and New Bank of India (later merged with Punjab National Bank)).

References

1. Rakesh Mohan, 'Ownership and governance of private sector banks', *Business Standard*, 14 December 2020, p. 13, https://csep.org/opinion-commentary/why-private-banks-their-ownership-structures-need-to-be-strictly-regulated/
2. Amol Agrawal, 'Why Indira Gandhi nationalised India's banks'. Bloomberg Quint, Opinion. 12 July 2019, www.bloombergquint.com/opinion/why-indira-gandhi-nationalised-indias-banks
3. Reserve Bank of India, Chronology of Events, 'Social controls, the nationalisation of banks, and the era of bank expansion – 1968 to 1985', www.rbi.org.in/scripts/chro_1968.aspx
4. On 10 February 1970 the Supreme Court held it void mainly on the grounds that it was discriminatory against the 14 banks and that the compensation proposed to be paid by Govt was not fair compensation. A fresh Ordinance was issued on 14 February which was later replaced by the Banking Companies (Acquisition and Transfer of Undertakings) Act, 1970 (5 of 1970). (Reserve Bank of India, Chronology of Events, 'Social controls, the nationalisation of banks, and the era of bank expansion – 1968 to 1985', www.rbi.org.in/scripts/chro_1968.aspx).
5. The Reserve Bank of India: 1967–1981, RBI Volume 3, 'The defining event', https://rbidocs.rbi.org.in/rdocs/content/PDFs/90069.pdf

6. Nilanjan Mukhopadhyay, 'Past continuous: How Indira Gandhi used presidential elections to cement her own power', *The Wire*, 25 May, 2017, https://thewire.in/history/indira-gandhi

7. Jairam Ramesh (2018). *'Intertwined Lives: PN Haksar and Indira Gandhi.* Simon & Schuster. India.

8. D. N. Ghosh (2015). *No Regrets.* Rupa Publications.

9. Jairam Ramesh (2019). 'July 19, 1969: Fifty years ago, India nationalised 14 private banks. This is how it was done', Scroll.in, 19 July, https://scroll. in/article/930982/july-19-1969-fifty-years-ago-india-nationalised-14-priv ate-banks-this-is-how-it-was-done .

10. Reserve Bank of India, Annual Report 2019–20, 'Credit delivery and financial inclusion', 25 August 2020, https://m.rbi.org.in/Scripts/ AnnualReportPublications.aspx?Id=1288

11. Kothari, S. P., 'Bank privatisation-make that withdrawal', *Economic Times*, 25 February 2021, p. 14.

12. Government of India, Budget 2021–2022, Speech of Nirmala I Sitharaman, Minister of Finance, 1 February 2021, www.indiabudget.gov.in/doc/ budget_speech.pdf

13. Nikunj Ohri, 'Govt backs NARCL with Rs 30,600-crore guarantee for five years', *Business Standard*, 17 September 2021, www.business-standard. com/article/economy-policy/govt-backs-narcl-with-rs-30-600-crore-guarantee-for-five-years-121091700050_1.html

14. Financial Times, 'Modi shatters taboo with plan to privatise state banks', 7 February 2021, www.ft.com/content/3c1fd8b4-a057-4f43-b734-8c9cd37d07fd

15. Reserve Bank of India's Internal Working Group recommendations to review extant ownership guidelines and corporate structure for Indian Private Sector Banks, RBI, 28 Nov. 2020. www.rbi.org.in/Scripts/BS_ PressReleaseDisplay.aspx?prid=50695

16. Rakesh Mohan, 'Ownership and governance of private sector banks – Part II', *Business Standard*, 15 December 2020, https://csep.org/opinion-com-mentary/ownership-and-governance-of-private-sector-banks/

17. Kothari, S. P., 'Bank privatisation – make that withdrawal,' *Economic Times*, 25 February 2021, p. 14.

18. PTI, 'Niti Aayog submits names of 2 PSU banks to be privatised to govt panel', *Business Standard*, 3 June 2021, www.business-standard.com/art-icle/finance/niti-aayog-submits-names-of-psu-banks-to-be-privatised-to-govt-panel-121060300814_1.html

19. Deepak Kargaonkar, 'Privatisation buzz lifts Indian Overseas Bank, Central Bank stocks by 20%', *Business Standard*, 22 June 2021, www. business-standard.com/article/markets/privatisation-buzz-lifts-indian-overseas-bank-central-bank-stocks-by-20-121062200006_1.html

11 IPO of life insurance company and privatisation of a general insurance company

Introduction

The Finance Minister while presenting the Union government budget for the FY 2022 announced the bringing of Initial Public Offer (IPO) of Life Insurance Corporation (LIC), and the privatisation of one general insurance company in the FY 2021–22. It also announced that the Government would bring amendment to the Insurance Act, 1938 to increase the permissible Foreign Direct Investment (FDI) limit from 49% to 74% and allow foreign ownership and control with safeguards. Under the new structure, the majority of Directors on the Board and key management persons would be resident Indians, with at least 50% of directors being independent directors, and specified percentage of profits being retained as general reserve.[1]

Nationalisation of insurance

Life insurance

First through an Ordinance of 19 January 1956, and then by law passed by the Parliament, the Life Insurance Act, 1956, the government nationalised 154 Indian,16 non-Indian insurers, and 75 provident societies into a single entity and LIC came into being on 1 September 1956.[2]

General insurance

The Parliament passed the General Insurance Business (Nationalisation) Act on 20 September 1972 nationalising general insurance business of 55 Indian companies and the undertakings of 52 foreign insurers. A month later, these 107 companies were amalgamated into four separate companies –National Insurance Company Ltd, Oriental Insurance Company Ltd, New India Assurance Company Ltd, and United India

DOI: 10.4324/9781003262213-12

Insurance Ltd. On 22 November 1972, General Insurance Corporation (GIC) was incorporated to control and run the business of general insurance. The Government transferred all its shares of the four companies to it, turning GIC into a holding company. Following the formation of Insurance Regulatory and Development Authority (IRDA) in April 2000, an amendment ended the monopoly GIC had over the general insurance. The amendment to the ACT – General Insurance Business 224 (Nationalisation) Amendment Act – turned GIC into a reinsurer, removed its supervisory role over the four subsidiaries and transferred the shares vested with it back to the government.[3]

In 2015, the Modi government introduced the Insurance Laws (Amendment) Bill – 2015 to replace the Insurance Act of 1938, General Insurance Business (Nationalisation) Act, 1972 and the Insurance Regulatory and Development Authority Act, 1999. The then Finance Minister, Arun Jaitley, while piloting the amendments assured Lok Sabha (House of the people) that LIC would continue as a fully-owned government entity while allowing disinvestment in state-owned general insurance companies: General Insurance Corporation (GIC Re), New India Assurance, United India Insurance, Oriental Insurance Company, and National Insurance Company. The government also added a new section – 10B – to the Act, according to which GIC Re and insurance companies could raise their capital for increasing their business in rural and social sectors to meet solvency margins and such other purposes as the central government deemed fit.[4]

The global insurance industry and India

According to Zurich-based reinsurers Swiss Re, report, 'World insurance: riding out the 2020 pandemic storm', India ranks 11 in the list of top 15 insurance markets in 2019 by total direct premium volume. India's global market share is 1.7% (vis-à-vis 0.4% in 1980), and its total premium volume is US $106 billion (vis-à-vis US $ 2 billion in 1980). The report forecasted that in 2030, India would increase its market share to 2.3% with total premium volume of US $ 234 billion. It would then rank at number 9 in top insurance markets globally.[5]

The Swiss Report estimated that in 2019, global premiums grew steadily at just below 3% in real terms. Life sector growth slowed to 2.2%, stronger than the 1.5% average of the previous ten years. At 3.5%, non-life premium growth in 2019 was slightly above the 10-year average. The emerging markets outperformed in both life and non-life.[6]

In emerging markets, life insurance had robust performance in Vietnam and India in 2019 which offset slower premium growth in other markets in the region. Life premiums in India grew by more than 7% in 2019. The government's focus on financial inclusion has also led to the introduction of premium subsidies for low income households. This boosted uptake in rural areas. However, non-life premium growth in India slowed to below 6% in 2019.[6]

For 2020, the report stated that the Covid-19 crisis will put global premium (life and non-life) growth back by around 3 percentage points. However, the combined life and non-life direct premiums written will recover to above pre-pandemic levels over the course of 2021.[6]

FDI increased in insurance sector

India had earlier allowed 49% FDI in insurance sector but the foreign insurance companies wanted to retain control with their capital. It was possible only if the FDI bar went up above 51% and preferably to 74%.

The government announced in the Union Budget 2021–22 to increase the permissible Foreign Direct Investment (FDI) limit from 49% to 74% in insurance companies and allow foreign ownership and control. This provides opportunities for both the life and non-life insurance companies in India that could deepen and widen the market for products.

Life Insurance Corporation (LIC)

LIC and its iconic logo has been a symbol of financial security for Indians born before the new millennium.[7] 290 million – or one in five – Indians are insured by the government-owned Life Insurance Corporation. It still controls 66% of the country's life insurance market even though private insurers were allowed in 1999 and have been around for over two decades. Despite the presence of many companies, the insurance penetration in the country has risen by only one percentage point in 16 years. It was 2.7% in 2001 and 3.7% in 2017.[8]

LIC is financially huge like no other public or private corporate in the country, overshadowing even the State Bank of India (SBI). It was the largest life insurer in the country with a total first-year premium of over ₹1.84 lakh crore in the year ended March 2021. It has 2.9 lakh employees, and a network of 22.78 lakh agents. As of 31 March 2020 it had total assets of ₹ 37.75 lakh crore and asset under management (AUM) of ₹ 6.63 lakh crore.[9]

LIC has certain inbuilt advantages that account for its continuing dominance. Unlike private insurance companies, LIC policies have a sovereign guarantee as envisaged under Section 37 of the LIC Act, 1956, giving it a higher level of trust. The Income Tax Act, 1961, as amended, gives a deduction up to ₹150,000 for those investing in life insurance policies under Section 80C. A lot of savings, therefore, get diverted to life insurance in India. Majority of the policies, LIC sells savings-cum-life cover. These products are 'participating' in nature. A 'participating' policy enables a policyholder to share the profits of the insurance company in the form of bonuses or dividends. Section 28 of the Life Insurance Corporation Act stipulates that 95% of the profits on valuation surplus be transferred to policyholders (after taxation), and the balance 5% to the government, as dividend.

Subsequent IRDAI regulations have reduced the stipulation to 90% to policyholders and 10% to the shareholder (the government); however, LIC is sticking to the old 95:5 formula to distribute the said surplus between policyholders and the government. In other words, under the Act, policyholders – not shareholders – have the first right to LIC's profits. What is given to the government is described as net profit, which also explains why LIC's retained profits (₹2,713 crore in 2019–20) and reserves are very low.[10] It would be interesting to watch whether this structure which is skewed towards policyholders in profit-sharing would change after IPO.

Despite these positives, the corporation has built up inefficiencies. The gross non-performing assets (NPA) ratio of the debt portfolio of Life Insurance Corporation of India (LIC) rose to an all-time high of 8.17% at the end of FY 2020. The gross NPA was 6.15% at the end of FY19. The net NPA ratio of the debt portfolio stood at 0.79% at the end of FY20. A year-ago, the net NPA ratio of debt portfolio was at 0.27%.[11]

IPO of LIC

The editor-in-chief of *India Today*, India's most read magazine, Aroon Purie wrote in the 22 March 2021 issue that for years, LIC was a no-go for disinvestment. Despite many attempts in the past, especially when the insurance sector was opened in 1999, the corporation has evaded listing or disinvestment. There are several reasons for this, not the least of which is the fact that, over the years, besides being an insurer, LIC has also functioned as the government's lender of the last resort. It has stepped in with its huge corpus to bail out state-run banks, subscribed to bonds floated by the government and met the state's disinvestment targets by buying up stakes in government firms. LIC's total investment portfolio as of March 2020 stood at ₹33.7 lakh crore, nearly four times the combined figure for private insurance companies.[12]

Hurdles to overcome before the IPO

The government had to amend the LIC Act, 1956 to facilitate the IPO. As many as 27 amendments were pushed through the Finance Bill 2021, tabled by the Finance Minister Nirmala Sitharaman along with Budget 2021–22. The amendments were passed in March 2021. These amendments were needed as the LIC Act did not have the provisions of listing on stock exchanges. The amendments will lead to setting up of a board with independent directors in line with listing obligations which ought to be fulfilled. Currently, the government owns 100% stake in LIC. Once listed, LIC is likely to become the country's biggest company by market capitalisation with an estimated valuation of ₹8–10 lakh crore.[13]

The government notified easier dilution norms in June 2021 for mega IPO. Companies with post-listing market capitalisation (m-cap) of more than ₹1 trillion will have to dilute ₹5,000 crore and at least 5% of their m-cap instead of earlier 10%.[14] Further, the government inserted a new rule in the public listing norms specified in the Securities Contracts (Regulation) Rules, 1957, by which it can now exempt any listed public sector enterprise from the minimum public shareholding norm, which mandates at least 25% public float for all listed entities. The move comes as the government prepares for the initial public offer (IPO) of Life Insurance Corp (LIC) of India, likely to be the biggest listing ever.[15]

The most crucial issue for the government is to find the right valuation before going to the capital markets. For life insurance firms like LIC, whose premium income is staggered over a long tenure, valuation involves the discovery of an embedded value. The government selected US based actuarial firm Milliman Advisors to ascertain the embedded value of LIC, while Deloitte and SBI Caps have been appointed as pre-IPO transaction advisors.[16,17]

Starting first with a small tranche of shares would help in discovery of price, as global experience suggest that subsequent tranches have yielded higher prices. A case in point is Nippon Telegraph and Telephone Corporation (NTT) which made the largest stock offering to date, in 1987 in three tranches. The first tranche in February 1987 was by far the largest equity issue in history. The second tranche in November 1987 was offered at a 150% premium over the price of the first tranche. The first two tranches were restricted to Japanese investors and were several times oversubscribed. The third tranche in October 1988 reduced the government equity to 65.4%. There have been further sale of NTT in tranches.[i] Another notable example we have dealt with in Chapter 4 is of ENI in Italy which divested its equity in tranches (1995,

I tranche – 15%; 1996, II tranche – 15.82%; 1997, III tranche –17.60%; 1998 IV tranche – 14.83%; 2001 V tranche – 5%). This resulted in privatisation of ENI to the extent of 68.25%.

There is a growing confidence in the Indian equity market among retail investors. Higher returns and greater liquidity, coupled with a low interest rate environment, have made equity markets attractive for the common investor despite Covid-19 pandemic. It is expected that the LIC IPO would be oversubscribed many fold. The government announcement that it will keep up to 10% of issue size in the IPO reserved for LIC policyholders would give the IPO further boost.[18]

The Securities and Exchange Board of India on 6 August 2021 also relaxed the lock-in period. Currently, 20% of the promoter shareholding – known as minimum contribution – is subject to a three-year lock-in, and the rest of the shareholding is locked for one year. The lock-in on minimum contribution would now be reduced to just 18 months if the IPO is entirely an offer for sale or where 50% of the issue proceeds are not meant for capital expenditure. This is likely to boost the sentiment of private equity (PE) investors.[19]

Besides giving much needed finances to the government, the IPO would bring a greater degree of transparency in LIC operations, disclosures, compliances, and accountability. For LIC, the challenge lies in bringing efficiency across the large agent network and in maintaining its market share.

Privatisation of general insurance

The Finance Minister introduced in Lok Sabha on Friday, 30 July 2021, the General Insurance Business (Nationalisation) Amendment Bill, 2021, which sought to remove the requirement that the central government holds not less than 51% of the equity capital in a specified insurer. Several opposition members opposed the introduction of the bill, saying it will bring in foreign investors and entail total privatisation of PSU general insurance companies. Refuting the charge, the FM stated that this is not to privatise insurance companies. We are bringing some enabling provision so that the Government can bring in public, Indian citizens, and common people's participation in the general insurance companies. Public-private participation in the general insurance industry will help get more resources, and enhance insurance penetration and social protection and better secure the interests of policyholders and contribute to faster growth of the economy.[20]

The government has not made a public announcement as to which of the four general insurance companies in the public sector – National

Insurance Company Limited, New India Assurance Company Limited, Oriental Insurance Company Limited, and the United India Insurance Company Limited would be privatised. However, it is understood that it is to be the United India Insurance Company Limited.

The Telegraph online reported on 6 August 2021 that the West Bengal Finance Minister Amit Mitra wrote to the Union Finance Minister urging to rethink on the government's plans to privatise public-sector insurance companies including the Life Insurance Corporation and the United India Insurance Company. He referred to the ₹11,396 crore invested by United India in government securities, government guaranteed bonds, and short-term treasury bills and said privatising the company would 'itself raise hydra-headed financial problems while undermining the confidence of the common retail insurers of the poorer sections of society'. Mitra said the same hold true for the LIC, underscoring that its volume of investment in the Indian economy stood at a 'staggering ₹36.76 lakh crore (FY 2020–21), out of which ₹23.75 lakh crore is in government securities'. Besides, the LIC's loans to the government, government bodies and corporate groups add up to more than ₹21,000 crore. Mitra added that 'Privatising LIC would lead to opening a Pandora's box, throwing into insecurity 30 crore (300 million) policyholders. Also, such privatisation of LIC would put into jeopardy the livelihoods of 12 to 15 lakh insurance agents. This will also throw into uncertainty the lives of 1.14 lakh employees.'[21] However, the bill was passed in Lok Sabha on Monday, 2 August 2021 amid opposition protests and sloganeering, without a debate.[22]

It would be interesting to watch how the disinvestment/privatisation of insurance sector would play out. Would it enhance insurance penetration, and social protection, and better secure the interests of policyholders, as claimed by the government. Or, as feared by opposition, it would raise hydra-headed financial problems, and make 30 crore (300 million) policyholders insecure besides putting into jeopardy the livelihoods of 12 to 15 lakh insurance agents and 1.14 lakh employees.

Note

i (Details can be seen at https://group.ntt/en/ir/shares/history.html.)

References

1. Government of India, Budget 2021–2022, Speech of NirmalaI Sitharaman, Minister of Finance, 1February 2021, www.indiabudget.gov.in/doc/budget_speech.pdf

2. Gautam Chikermane (2018), *70 Policies that Shaped India,* Observer Research Foundation, pp. 29–30. www.orfonline.org/wp-content/uploads/2018/07/70_Policies.pdf

3. Gautam Chikermane (2018), *70 Policies that Shaped India,* Observer Research Foundation, pp. 53–4. www.orfonline.org/wp-content/uploads/2018/07/70_Policies.pdf

4. Sitanshu Swain, 'Unlocking LIC's value', *India Today,* 22 March 2021, 12–23. www.indiatoday.in/magazine/cover-story/story/20210322-unlocking-lic-s-value-1778914-2021-03-14

5. Swiss Re, Sigma No. 4/2020 ' World insurance: riding out the 2020 pandemic storm', Table 2, p. 10, www.swissre.com/dam/jcr:05ba8605-48d3-40b6-bb79-b891cbd11c36/sigma4_2020_en.pdf

6. Swiss Re, Sigma No. 4/2020 'World insurance: riding out the 2020 pandemic storm', www.swissre.com/dam/jcr:05ba8605-48d3-40b6-bb79-b891cbd11c36/sigma4_2020_en.pdf

7. The LIC logo is two hands gently circling the lamp and below it two words are written in Sanskrit 'Yogakshemam Vahamyaham' which means 'I shall ensure the safety and well-being of my devotees' (as told by Lord Krishna to his devotees in Bhagavadgita, Chapter 9, verse 22).

8. Kishor Kadam, 'Insurance penetration in India grows just 1% in last one and half decade; These six charts explain why', *Firstpost,* 25 January 2019, www.firstpost.com/business/insurance-penetration-in-india-grows-just-1-in-last-one-and-half-decade-these-six-charts-explain-why-5953351.html

9. George Mathew and Sandeep Singh, 'Explained: LIC's IPO and its customers', *Indian Express,* 23 July 2021, https://indianexpress.com/article/explained/lics-ipo-and-its-customers-7417712/

10. Sitanshu Swain, ' Unlocking LIC's value', *India Today,* 22 March 2021, 12–23, www.indiatoday.in/magazine/cover-story/story/20210322-unlocking-lic-s-value-1778914-2021-03-14

11. M. Saraswathy, 'LIC's gross NPA ratio in debt portfolio at record high of 8.17% at end of FY20', *Moneycontrol,* 6 August 2020, www.moneycontrol.com/news/business/economy/lics-gross-npa-ratio-in-debt-portfolio-at-record-high-of-8-17-at-end-of-fy20-5648671.html

12. Aroon Purie, 'From the Editor-in-Chief', *India Today,* 22 March 2021, p. 3, www.indiatoday.in/magazine/editor-s-note/story/20210322-from-the-editor-in-chief-1778920-2021-03-14

13. PTI, 'Finance Bill proposes 27 amendments in LIC Act', 3 February 2021, https://bfsi.economictimes.indiatimes.com/news/insurance/finance-bill-proposes-27-amendments-in-lic-act/80662429

14. Ruchika Chitravanshi and Samie Modak, 'Easier dilution norms in play for mega IPOs', *Business Standard,* 20 June 2021, www.business-standard.com/article/markets/easier-dilution-norms-for-large-ipos-where-post-listing-m-cap-tops-rs-1-trn-121062000460_1.html

15. The Economic Times, 'Government can exempt any listed PSU from min-imum public holding', 1 August 2021, https://economictimes.indiatimes.com/news/economy/policy/govt-can-exempt-any-listed-psu-from-min-public-holding/articleshow/84929409.cms?from=mdr

16. Hindu Businessline, 'LIC IPO: Govt appoints Milliman Advisors to determine "embedded value" of the insurer', 31 December 2020, www.thehindubusinessline.com/markets/stock-markets/lic-ipo-govt-appoints-milliman-advisors-to-find-embedded-value-of-the-insurer/article33463908.ece

17. Moneycontrol, 'LIC IPO: Govt clears appointment of SBI Caps, Deloitte as pre-listing transaction Advisors', 22 August 2020, www.moneycontrol.com/news/business/lic-ipo-govt-clears-appointment-of-sbi-caps-deloitte-as-pre-listing-transaction-advisors-5739861.html

18. Business Today, '10% of LIC IPO issue size to be reserved for policyholders', 9 February 2021, www.businesstoday.in/latest/economy-politics/story/lic-policyholders-to-have-an-advantage-during-ipo-launch-heres-how-287033-2021-02-09

19. Samie Modak, 'Sebi halves the post-IPO lock-in period for promoters to 18 months', *Business Standard*, 7 August 2021, www.business-standard.com/article/markets/sebi-halves-the-post-ipo-lock-in-period-for-promoters-to-18-months-121080601554_1.html

20. Press Trust of India, 'Bill to amend general insurance law introduced in Lok Sabha', *Business Standard*, 30 July 2021, www.business-standard.com/article/economy-policy/bill-to-amend-general-insurance-law-introduced-in-lok-sabha-121073000708_1.html

21. Anita Joshua, 'Amit Mitra asks FM to reconsider LIC and United India Insurance Company's privatisation', The Telegraph online, 6 August 2021, www.telegraphindia.com/india/amit-mitra-asks-fm-to-reconsider-lic-and-united-india-insurance-companys-privatisation/cid/1824887

22. Special Correspondent, 'Lok Sabha passes Bill to amend insurance Act amid protests', *The Hindu*, 2 August 2021. www.thehindu.com/news/national/lok-sabha-passes-bill-to-amend-public-sector-general-insurance-law/article35679559.ece

12 Telecom sector – BSNL and MTNL

Introduction

Among the top ten loss-making CPSEs from the past few years, Bharat Sanchar Nigam Limited (BSNL), Mahanagar Telephone Nigam Limited (MTNL), and Air India have the ignominy to occupy the top three positions.

Bharat Sanchar Nigam Limited (BSNL)

BSNL was formed on 1 October 2000 by corporatisation of the earlier Department of Telecom Operations and Department Telecom Services. The company took over the erstwhile functions of the Department of Telecom in respect of provision of telecom services across the country excluding Delhi and Mumbai. In these two metropolitan cities, MTNL was providing services. In 2000, a national long-distance service and in 2012 an international long-distance calling service was opened to the private sector. Telecom giants, such as Vodafone, Airtel, Idea, and recently Reliance Jio entered the field in direct competition with BSNL. While these companies could acquire the 4G auctions and are currently exploring the possibility of 5G, BSNL is still struggling to get to 4G.

Writing in *Economic & Political Weekly*, Abraham and Jain noted that while the market share of private players in telecom services rose steeply from 39% in 2004 to almost 89% in 2019, the BSNL share declined steeply both in landline connections from 184.88 lakh in 2014 to 111.68 lakh in 2019 and in the mobile segment from 11.3% in 2012 to 10.6%. The private companies were spending only a fraction of revenues on wages and salaries as opposed to BSNL with 1.6 lakh employee workforce (as of 2019) whose salaries and benefits accounted for more than 53% of the revenue expenditure. The profit-making BSNL turned red since 2008–09. In 2019, BSNL was out of place and out of time.[1]

DOI: 10.4324/9781003262213-13

On 3 February 2021, the Minister of State for Telecom, Sanjay Dhotre informed Lok Sabha that BSNL's loss has swollen from ₹14,904 crore in 2018–19 to ₹15,500 crore in 2019–20.[2]

Mahanagar Telephone Nigam Limited (MTNL)

Mahanagar Telephone Nigam Limited (MTNL) was incorporated on 28 February 1986 under the Companies Act as a wholly owned Government company to provide services in the two Metropolitan Cities of Delhi and Mumbai. At that time telecom infrastructure in the country was extremely poor. MTNL emerged as one of the most valuable public sector companies and was given Navratna status in 1997. But then the downfall began. Most other operators had expanded to get a national footprint. MTNL had to go for expensive roaming agreements and other arrangements like points of interconnection to enable its users in Delhi and Mumbai to get pan-India network.

The Minister of State for Telecom informed Lok Sabha on 3 February 2021, that MTNL's loss has increased to ₹ 3,811 crore in 2019–20 from ₹3,398 crore in 2018–19.[2]

Efforts to merge BSNL and MTNL

Earlier efforts

Earlier in 2002, the then Communications Minister, Pramod Mahajan came up with the idea to merge MTNL and BSNL. The merger didn't go through due to structural complexities. MTNL is listed and BSNL is not so there was an issue of whether MTNL should be delisted or BSNL should be listed. At present, 56.25% equity shares of MTNL are held by Government of India, and remaining 43.75% shares are held by foreign institutional investors, financial institutions, banks, mutual funds, and others including individual investors.

The Parliamentary Committee on Review of Loss Making CPSUs for 2018–19, in its 24th report (submitted on 20 December 2018) noted that the government is considering merger of BSNL and MTNL, the two biggest loss-making PSEs in the communication sector. The Committee cautioned that in the backdrop of the fact that in a very similar scenario, the Government's decision to merge two heavy loss-making PSEs, Indian Airlines, and Air India didn't work very well. It opined that the Government should analyse all factors before taking any decision on the merger of MTNL and BSNL whose combined financial liabilities during 2016–17 was a whopping ₹24,038.73 crore, and the combined manpower of both PSUs is a staggering figure of 224,367 persons.[3]

Government revival plan of BSNL and MTNL, and merger

BSNL and MTNL have been bleeding money for years as competition from private players intensified in recent years after the arrival of Reliance Jio which undercut the market with its 4G telecom network, free voice calls, and incredibly low-cost data prices. Incumbents Vodafone and Airtel had to lower their prices and expand their 4G networks across the country. Both BSNL and MTNL have been demanding spectrum to start 4G services to remain competitive in the market.

On October 23,2019, the telecom minister Ravi Shankar Prasad informed in a press conference that the Union Cabinet has given its in-principle approval to the merger of BSNL and MTNL and plans to spend ₹ 69,000 crore to revive loss-making state-funded telecom operators Bharat Sanchar Nigam Ltd (BSNL) and Mahanagar Telephone Nigam Ltd (MTNL).[4]

The revival plan included infusion of ₹ 20,140 crore capital for purchase of 4G spectrum, ₹3,674 crore for GST to be paid on spectrum allocation, companies raising ₹15,000 crore in debt on the sovereign guarantee and government funding ₹17,160 crore voluntary retirement scheme (VRS) and another ₹12,768 crore towards retirement liability. The two firms will monetise assets worth ₹37,500 crore in the next three years. MTNL, which is a listed company, will become a subsidiary of BSNL until the merger is completed,

Prasad told journalists that neither BSNL nor MTNL are being closed, nor are they being disinvested or being hived off to third party. The existence of BSNL, which alone serves more than 116 million subscribers, is in the strategic interest of the nation, Prasad added, 'Whenever we have flood or cyclone, BSNL is the first one to offer services for free.'[5] The Telecom Minister directed BSNL, and MTNL to proceed quickly on VRS, and Asset monetisation plans.[6]

To ease the wage costs, both BSNL and MTNL announced a VRS for its employees in November 2019. The option for VRS was opened for 30 days till 3 December 2019. The idea of the scheme was to restructure the company by shedding surplus labour and freeing up real estate, thus leading to monetisation of assets in the future. According to the plan, all permanent employees who are 50 years and above as on 31 January 2020, were eligible for opting for the VRS.

The Minister of State for Telecom Sanjay Dhotre in a written reply to Lok Sabha on 3 February 2021 informed that 78,569 employees of BSNL and 14,387 of MTNL opted for VRS which would lead to about 50% reduction of salary expenditure in BSNL and by about 75% in MTNL.[7]

As per the audited financial results for the year ending 31 March 2020, the total liabilities of BSNL and MTNL were ₹87,618 crore and ₹30,242 crore respectively. Also, they have not cleared their past adjusted gross revenue (AGR) dues of over ₹10,000 crore as calculated by the Department of Telecom. AGR liability of BSNL was to the tune of ₹5,835 crore and for MTNL it was around ₹4,352 crore up to financial year 2016–17, which includes interest, penalty, and interest on penalty.[8]

Minister of State for Communications Devusinh Chauhan in a written reply to a question in the Rajya Sabha on 5 August 2021 submitted that the BSNL loss has narrowed to ₹7,441 crore in 2020–21 from ₹15,500 in 2019–20. MTNL also reported a total loss of ₹2,554 crore for the last fiscal year, compared to ₹3,811 crore in 2019–20, Chauhan added. The data shared by Chauhan showed that total liabilities of BSNL have come down to ₹81,156 crore in 2020–21, from ₹87,618 crore in 2019–20. The total liabilities of MTNL have reduced to ₹29,391 crore from ₹30,242 crore between the reported fiscal years.

BSNL and MTNL however, lags in terms of mobile towers compared to its private sector competitors. Whereas BSNL has 153,628 base transceiver stations (BTS) and MTNL has 4,242 BTS, the country's largest mobile player Reliance Jio has 930,390 BTS, which is six times more than the number of BTS of the public sector firms. Airtel has 622,087 BTS, which is four times, and Vodafone Idea has 529,529 BTSs which are over three times compared to mobile antenna sites of BSNL and MTNL combined.[9]

The Government defers BSNL–MTNL merger

But the much hyped merger of BSNL and MTNL was put on hold. The Group of Ministers (GOM) in its meeting on 25 January 2021 deferred merger of MTNL and BSNL mainly due to high debt of MTNL. Besides debt, there were issues around salary structure between BSNL and MTNL employees and bringing them on par with each other was a challenge. While deferring the merger of telecom PSUs, the GOM approved allocation of 4G spectrum to BSNL in Delhi and Mumbai in place of MTNL.[10]

BSNL was given a licence by the Department of Telecom (DoT) to operate the mobile network of MTNL as its outsourced agency in Mumbai and Delhi from 1 January 2021.[11]

According to TRAI data released for the year ending 31 March 2021, the wire line broadband base of BSNL stood at 6.82 million, followed by 3.09 million of Airtel, 2.60 million of Jio, 1.85 million of ACT (Atria Convergence Technologies) and 1.07 million of Hathway Cable. In wireless broadband, there is huge competition. Jio's base stood at 422.92 million, followed by Airtel at 188.84 million, Vi at 123.60 million.[12]

National Monetisation Pipeline: BSNL and MTNL

The National Monetisation Pipeline (NMP) of potential brownfield infrastructure assets prepared by NITI Aayog was issued by the Union Finance Minister on 23August 2021. The NMP is co-terminus with the remaining four-year period of the National Infrastructure Pipeline (NIP) from FY 2022 to FY2025. In the telecom sector 2.86 lakh km of Bharatnet fibre (57% of the asset base) and 14,917 number of towers of BSNL and MTNL (21% of towers) with indicative monetisation value of ₹35,100 crore (₹26,300 crore from Bharatnet Fibre, and ₹8,800 crore from BSNL and MTNL towers) are planned to be monetised. This represents 6% of overall NMP in value terms during FY 2022 to FY2025.[13]

Bharatnet optical fibre

About 286,255 km of existing fibre assets of Bharat Broadband Network Limited (BBNL) and Bharat Sanchar Nigam Ltd (BSNL) spanning over 16 states has been considered for monetisation through PPP mode. The Bharatnet project is the backbone of 'Digital India' and aims to reduce the digital divide between urban and rural India. The project involves laying of optical fibre cable between block and gram panchayats. This infrastructure would be made available to service providers who, in turn, would utilise it to provide affordable high speed broadband to rural citizens and institutions. There are 2.53 lakh gram panchayats as per Ministry of Panchayati Raj, Government of India, 'Basic Statistics of Panchayati Raj Institutions' (2019). As of 19 March 2021, about 5.13 lakh km of optical fibre cable laying has been completed covering 1.57 lakh gram panchayats. The project is proposed to be implemented through Develop, Build, Finance, Operate, and Maintain (DBFOT) model under PPP mode.

Telecom towers

About 14,900 towers of BSNL and MTNL (~13,567 towers of BSNL and ~1,350 towers of MTNL) with co-locations from third party telecom operators are being considered for monetisation during

FY2023. Rent–Operate–Transfer (ROT) concession model akin to the model employed by NHAI in the roads sector is proposed. The right to rent, operate, and maintain the tower rentals will be granted to a concessionaire for a pre-defined concession period as against an upfront consideration, which could be the bidding parameter.

Selling of land assets of BSNL and MTNL

The land assets of BSNL,and MTNL along with some other Public Sector Undertakings land parcels are being considered for sale via e-bidding. Unlike the asset monetisation plan under NMP, the ownership of lands will be transferred to the new owner (*Business Standard*, 3 September 2021).[14]

The Union Cabinet approved on 15 September 2021, a relief package for the stressed telecom sector that includes a four-year break from paying statutory dues, permission to share scarce airwaves, change in the definition of revenue on which levies are paid (non-telecom revenue will be excluded on prospective basis from the definition of Adjusted Gross Revenue (AGR)), and allowing 100% foreign investment through the automatic route.[15]

References

1. Vinoj Abraham and Ritika Jain, 'Privatisation and the Voluntary Retirement Scheme, The case of BSNL', *Economic & Political Weekly* 55(40), 3 Oct, 2020.
2. The Hindu Businessline, 'Why merging BSNL and MTNL is a good idea', 23 October 2019, www.thehindubusinessline.com/info-tech/why-merging-bsnl-and-mtnl-is-a-good-idea/article29777772.ece
3. Twenty-fourth report, Committee on Public Undertakings (2018–19) (Sixteenth Lok Sabha), Review of Loss Making CPSUs, Ministry of Heavy Industries and Public Enterprises (Department of Public Enterprises), http://164.100.47.193/lsscommittee/Public%20Undertakings/16_Public_Undertakings_24.pdf5.
4. Nikunj Ohri, 'Cabinet gives in-principle approval to merge BSNL, MTNL', *Blooomberg Quint*, 23 October 2019, www.bloombergquint.com/business/cabinet-gives-in-principle-approval-to-merge-bsnl-mtnl
5. PTI. 'BSNL, MTNL to merge under Rs 69,000 cr revival plan; 4G spectrum, VRS part of scheme', *Business Standard*, 23 October 2019, www.business-standard.com/article/pti-stories/bsnl-mtnl-to-merge-under-rs-69-000-cr-revival-plan-4g-spectrum-vrs-part-of-scheme-119102301538_1.html
6. PTI, 'Telecom Minister directs BSNL, MTNL to proceed quickly on VRS, asset monetisation plans', *Bloomberg Quint*, 3 November 2019,

www.bloombergquint.com/business/prasad-directs-bsnl-mtnl-to-proceed-quickly-on-vrs-asset-monetisation-plans

7. Malvika Gurung,'BSNL lost Rs 15,500 crore this year, will Govt shut it down? Here's official reply from Minister', Trak.in, 5 February 2021, https://trak.in/tags/business/2021/02/05/bsnl-lost-rs-15500-crore-this-year-will-govt-shut-it-down-heres-official-reply-from-minister/

8. PTI, 'BSNL, MTNL have not cleared AGR dues of over Rs 10,000 cr yet', *Business Today*, 8 April 2021, www.businesstoday.in/sectors/telecom/bsnl-mtnl-have-not-cleared-agr-dues-of-over-rs-10000-cr-yet/story/436126.html

9. Press Trust of India, 'State-owned BSNL, MTNL narrow losses, reduce liabilities in 2020–21', *Business Standard*, 5 August 2021, www.business-standard.com/article/companies/state-owned-bsnl-mtnl-narrow-losses-reduce-liabilities-in-2020-21-121080501442_1.html

10. PTI, 'GoM defers BSNL–MTNL merger; approves BSNL land sale to CBSE for Rs 64 cror', *Financial Express*, 25 January 2021, www.financialexpress.com/industry/gom-defers-bsnl-mtnl-merger-approves-bsnl-land-sale-to-cbse-for-rs-64-crore/2178667/

11. Yasmin Ahmed, 'BSNL starts telecom operations in Delhi and Mumbai, takes over MTNL's mobile network', *India Today*, 4 January 2021, www.indiatoday.in/technology/news/story/bsnl-starts-telecom-operations-in-delhi-and-mumbai-takes-over-mtnl-s-mobile-network-1755771-2021-01-04

12. Kiran Rathee, 'Reliance Jio adds maximum users among telecom operators for second consecutive month', *Financial Express*, 19 June 2021, www.financialexpress.com/industry/reliance-jio-adds-maximum-users-among-telecom-operators-for-second-consecutive-month/2274163/

13. NITI Aayog, National Monetisation Pipeline, Volume II: Asset Pipeline, pp. 45–50. www.niti.gov.in/sites/default/files/2021-08/Vol_2_NATIONAL_MONETISATION_PIPELINE_23_Aug_2021.pdf

14. Nikunj Ohri, 'Centre plans PSU land sale worth more than Rs 600 crore via e-bidding', 3 September 2021, www.business-standard.com/article/economy-policy/centre-plans-psu-land-sale-worth-more-than-rs-600-crore-via-e-bidding-121090300049_1.html

15. Business Standard, 'Telecom reforms usher in new era for India's digital ambitions: Telcos',   www.business-standard.com/article/companies/telecom-reforms-usher-in-new-era-for-india-s-digital-ambitions-telcos-121091501436_1.html

Appendix A

Table A.1 CPSE disinvestment: Target and achievement (1991–92 to 2020–21) (in crores of ₹)

Year	Target	Realisation-Government Sources	Realisation-BSE PSU data	Methodology
1991–92	2,500	3,038	3,038	Minority shares of 30 enterprises sold by auction method in bundles of 'very good', 'good', and average, in two tranches. (AY, BEML, BEL, BHEL, BPCL, BRPL, CRL, CMC, DCI, FACT, HMT, HOCL, HPCL, HPF, HZL, HCL, IPCL, IRCON, ITI, MRL, MTNL, MMTC, NALCO, NFL, NLC, RCFL, SCI, STC, SAIL, VSNL).
1992–93	2,500	1,913	1,913	Minority equity sold by auction method separately for 16 enterprises (14 enterprises were disinvested in 1991–92 also). Hindustan Copper Ltd and NMDC were other two.
1993–94	3,500	–	–	An advertisement for sale of shares was released in March 1994. Actual realisation of funds from this round of disinvestment took place in 1994–95.
1994–95	4,000	4,843	4,843	In all, disinvestment proceeds of 16 enterprises realised of which 9 were disinvested in 1991–92 also. The 7 enterprises which were disinvested for the first time: CONCOR, IOC, ONGC, EIL, GAIL, ITDC, and Kudremukh Iron Ore Ltd.
1995–96	7,000	168*	168*	Equity of 4 companies which were partially disinvested earlier (MTNL, SAIL, CONCOR, ONGC) auctioned realising ₹168 crore…In addition, shares of IDBI were disinvested for ₹193 crore. PSEs Survey does not include this amount. However, Ministry of Finance includes this as disinvestment proceeds.*

(*continued*)

Table A.1 Cont.

Year	Target	Realisation-Government Sources	Realisation-BSE PSU data	Methodology
1996–97	5,000	380	380	GDR of VSNL in international market
1997–98	4,800	902	910	GDR of MTNL in international market
2000–01	10,000	1,869	1,871	BALCO, KRL (CRL), and MRL through strategic sale/acquisition
2001–02	12,000	3,131	3,268	Strategic sale of CMC, HTL, IBP, VSNL, and PPL. Sale of 8 hotels and long-term lease of 1 hotel of ITDC.
2002–03	12,000	3,265	2,348	Strategic sale of HZL, IPCL, Maruti Udyog Ltd. Sale of 10 ITDC properties and residual equity of MFIL.
2003–04	14,500	15,547	15,547	
2004–05	4,000	2,765	2,765	
2005–06	No Target	1,570	1,570	
2006–07	No Target	–	–	
2007–08	No Target	4,181	4,181	
2008–09	No Target	–	–	
2009–10	25,000	23,553	23,553	Methodology followed was mainly Initial Public Offer (IPO) and Follow-On Public Offer (FPO)
2010–11	40,000	22,144	22,763	Methodology followed was mainly Initial Public Offer (IPO) and Follow-On Public Offer (FPO)
2011–12	40,000	13,894	14,035	Methodology followed was Follow-On Public Offer (FPO) and Offer For Sale (OFS)
2012–13	30,000	22,957	23,857	Methodology followed was Follow-On Public Offer (FPO) and Offer For Sale (OFS)
2013–14	54,000	15,819	21,321	Methodology followed was Buyback of shares, Block Deal, FPO, Employee OFS, Cross holding by Oil CPSEs, and Institutional Placement Programme (IPP).

2014–15	58,425	24,349	24,349	Variety of above methods used
2015–16	69,500	23,997	24,058	Variety of above methods used
2016–17	56,500	46,247	46,378	Besides other methods, Exchange Traded Fund method used by creating CPSEs basket of equity.
2017–8	72,500	100,057	100,642	Methodologies included OFS, Buyback, IPO, and disinvestment of strategic holding in Specified Understanding of the Unit Trust of India (SUUTI), HPCL-ONGC off market deal, and IPO of insurance companies GIC and NIA.
2018–19	80,000	84,972	85,063	Methodologies included strategic sale of DCL, NPCC, PFC-REC deal, CPSE ETF, Bharat 22 ETF, SUUTI sale of Axis Bank shares, and minority stake in other PSEs.
2019–20	90,000	50,299	49,828	Methodologies included strategic sale of Kamarajar Port Ltd, NEEPCO, THDC, CPSE-ETF, Bharat 22 ETF, IPO, OFS, Buy back, remittances from SUUTI, and sale of enemy shares.
2020–21	2,10,000	32,835	30,213	Predominant Methodologies remained Exchange Traded Fund, Buy Back, CPSE to CPSE sale and also included some strategic sale of private equity.
2021–22	1,75,000			
TOTAL		5,18,044	515,818	

Source: Created by author based on Government data: Ministry of Disinvestment website and DIPAM website (from 2009–10 onwards) www.dipam. gov.in/dipam/past-disinvestment, and BSE PSU data – http://bsepsu.com/disinvest_database.asp#prettyPhoto[iframe]/9/, accessed 19 May 2021

Appendix B: Recommendations of disinvestment commissions
(Commission Report, Year)

1. Air India Ltd(AI) (Report VIII, August 1998)
2. Andrew Yule and Company (AYCL) (Report XXIV, September 2002)
3. Bharat Aluminum Company Limited (BALCO) (Report II, April 1997)
4. Bharat Heavy Electricals Ltd (BHEL) (Report XII, August 1999)
5. Bongaigaon Refineries and Petrochemicals Limited (BRPL) (Had already disinvested 24.54%) (Report II, April 1997))
6. Brahmputra Valley Fertilizer Corporation Ltd (BVFCL) (Report XX, May 2003)
7. Central Electronics Ltd (CEL) (Report VIII, August 1998)
8. Central Cottage Industries Corporation of India Ltd (CCIC) (Report XXII, September 2003)
9. Central Inland Water Transportation Corporation Ltd (CIWTC) (Report XIV, September 2002)
10. Central Mine Planning and Design Institute (CMPDIL) (Report XVIII, March 2003)
11. Central Warehousing Corporation (CWC) (Report XXV, March 2004)
12. Cochin Shipyard Ltd (Report XIV, September 2002)
13. Container Corporation of India Limited (CONCOR) (Had already disinvested 23.07%). (Report III, May 1997)
14. Cotton Corporation of India Ltd (CCI), (Report XVI, December 2002)
15. Dredging Corporation of India Ltd (DCI), (Report XV, November 2002)
16. Educational Consultants India Ltd (EdCIL), (Report XXIV, January 2004)
17. Electronics Corporation of India Ltd (ECIL), (Report XXIII, December 2003)

18. Electronics Trade and Technology Development Corporation (ET&T), (Report VI, December 1997)
19. Encore Port Ltd (Report XXIII, December 2003)
20. Fertiliser and Chemicals (Travancore) Ltd (FACT), (Report VII, March 1998)
21. Gas Authority of India Limited (GAIL), (Report I, February 1997)
22. Handicrafts and Handlooms Exports Corporation of India Ltd (HHEC). (Report XIX, April 2003)
23. Hindustan Copper Limited (HCL) (Report IV, August 1997)
24. Hindustan Insecticides Ltd (HIL) (Report XII, August 1999)
25. Hindustan Latex Ltd (HLL), (Report VII, March 1998)
26. Hindustan Organic Chemicals Ltd (HOCL), (Report XII, August 1999)
27. Hindustan Prefab Limited (HPL) (Report V, November 1997)
28. Hindustan Steel Works Construction Ltd (HSCL), (Report IX, March 1999)
29. Hindustan Teleprinters Limited (HTL), (Report II, April 1997)
30. Hindustan Vegetable Oils Corporation Ltd (HVOC), (Report VI, December 1997)
31. Hindustan Zinc Ltd (HZL), was already disinvested 24.08% ((Report VI, December 1997)
32. Hindustan Shipyard Ltd (HSL) (Report XIV, September 2002)
33. Hooghly Dock and Port Engineers Ltd (HDPE), (Report XVII, January 2003)
34. Hotel Corporation of India Ltd (HCIL), (Report VI, December 1997)
35. IBP Limited (IBP), (Report V, November 1997)
36. Indian Medicines Pharmaceuticals Ltd (Report XVI, December 2002)
37. Indian Petrochemicals Corp. Ltd (IPCL), (Report VII, March 1998)
38. IRCON International Ltd (IRCON), (Report XIV, September 2002)
39. Indian Telephone Industries (ITI) (Report II, April 1997)
40. Indian Vaccines Corporation Ltd (IVCOL), (Report XXIV, January 2004)
41. Indian Tourism Development Corporation (ITDC), (Report I, February 1997)
42. Jute Corporation of India Ltd (JCI), (Report XVI, December 2002)
43. Karnataka Antibiotics and Pharmaceuticals Ltd (KAPL) (Report XVIII, March 2003)
44. Kudremukh Iron Ore Company Limited (KIOCL), (Report III, May 1997)

45. Madras Fertilisers Ltd (MFL), (Report II, April 1997)
46. Mahanagar Telephone Nigam Limited (MTNL) (Had already disinvested including dilution of equity by Public Issue/GDR 43.80%), (Report III, May 1997)
47. Manganese Ore India Limited (MOIL) (Report II, April 1997) and Report XIII, January 2002)
48. Metal Scrap Trading Corp. Ltd (MSTC), (Report XI, July 1999)
49. Metallurgical & Engineering Consultants (India) Ltd (MECON), (Report XI, July 1999)
50. Mineral Exploration Corp Ltd (MECL), (Report XI, July 1999)
51. Minerals & Metals Trading Corporation of India Ltd (MMTC), (Report X, June 1999)
52. Modern Food Industries India Limited (MFIL) (Report I, February 1997)
53. National Aluminium Co. Ltd (NALCO), (Report VII, March 1998)
54. National Buildings Construction Corporation Ltd (NBCC), (Report XVI, December 2002)
55. National Film Development Corporation (NFDC), (Report XXI, July 2003)
56. National Fertiliser Ltd (NFL), (Report VII, March 1998)
57. National Handloom Development Corporation (NHDC), (Report XXII, September 2003
58. National Projects Construction Corporation Ltd (NPCC), (Report XV, November 2002)
59. National Hydro-electric Power Corporation Ltd (NHPC), (Report VI, December 1997)
60. National Small Industries Corporation Ltd (NSIC). (Report XVII, January 2003)
61. National Mineral Development Corp. Ltd (NMDC), (Report X, June 1999)
62. National Seeds Corporation Ltd (NSCL), (Report XX, May 2003)
63. National Thermal Power Corporation (NTPC), (Report V, November 1997)
64. NEPA Ltd (NEPA), (Report V, November 1997)
65. Neyveli Lignite Corporation Ltd (NLC), (Report VII, March 1998, and Report XIII, January 2002)
66. North Eastern Electric Power Corporation Ltd (NEEPCO), (Report XXII, September 2003)
67. North Eastern Handicrafts and Handlooms Corporation Ltd (NEHHDC), (Report XXIII, December 2003)
68. Numaligarh Refinery Ltd (NRL), (Report XXV, March 2004)
69. Oil India Limited (OIL), (Report III, May 1997)

70. Oil and Natural Gas Corporation Ltd (ONGC), (Report III, May 1997, and Report X, June 1999)
71. Paradeep Phosphates Ltd (PPL) (Report X, June 1999)
72. Pawan Hans Helicopters Ltd (Report IV, August 1997)
73. Power Finance Corporation (PFC), (Report XXI, July 2003)
74. Power Grid Corporation of India Limited (POWERGRID), (Report IV, August 1997)
75. Projects & Equipment Corporation Ltd (PEC), (Report X, June 1999) and Report XIII, January 2002)
76. Pyrites Phosphates & Chemicals Ltd [PPCL], (Report VI, December 1997)
77. .Rajasthan Drugs and Pharmaceuticals Ltd (RDPL) (Report XVII, January 2003)
78. Rail India Technical & Economic Services Ltd (RITES), (Report III, May 1997 & Report XIII, January 2002)
79. Ranchi Ashok Bihar Corporation, (Report V, November 1997)
80. Rashtriya Chemicals and Fertilisers Ltd (RCFL), (Report XII, August 1999)
81. Rashtriya Ispat Nigam Ltd (RINL), (Report XII, August 1999)
82. Rehabilitation Industries Corporation Ltd (RICL), (Report VI, December 1997)
83. Rural Electrification Corporation Ltd (REC), (Report XIX, April 2003)
84. Semiconductor Complex Ltd (SCL), (Report XV, November 2002)
85. Shipping Corporation of India Limited (SCI), (Report IV, August 1997)
86. Steel Authority of India Ltd (SAIL), (Report VII, March 1998)
87. State Farms Cooperation of India Ltd (SFCIL) (Report XIX, April 2003)
88. State Trading Corporation (STC), (Report IX, March 1999)
89. Telecommunications Consultants India Ltd (TCIL) (Report XV, November 2002
90. Sponge Iron India Limited (SIIL) (Report XI, July 1999)
91. Utkal Ashok Hotel Corporation Ltd (Report V, November 1997)
92. Water and Power Consultancy Services (India) Ltd (WAPCOS), (Report XXI, July 2003

Source: Created by author based on twenty-five reports of the Disinvestment Commission I and Disinvestment Commission II Reports.

Appendix C: Methodologies used for disinvestment of CPSEs

1. **Strategic disinvestment** refers to sale of substantial portion of the Government shareholding of a CPSE of up to 50%, or such higher percentage as the competent authority may determine, along with transfer of management control.

2. **Initial public offer** refers to offer of shares by an unlisted CPSE or the Government out of its shareholding or a combination of both to the public for subscription for the first time. Issue of fresh equity in conjunction with the sale of Government's stake is termed as piggy-back transaction.

   Offer for sale refers to sale of shares by the Government (promoter) through Stock Exchange mechanism. This method allows auction of shares on the platform provided by the Stock Exchange.

   New fund offer refers to disinvestment through Exchange Traded Fund (ETF) route, which allows simultaneous sale of Government's stake in various CPSEs across diverse sectors through a single offering. It provides a mechanism for the Government to monetise its shareholding in those CPSEs which form part of the ETF basket.

3. **CPSE to CPSE sale** refers to transactions involving sales made by the Government of one CPSE to another CPSE.

4. **Auction to financial investors** refers to transactions involving sales made by the Government in CPSEs through an auction to defined financial investors/investor groups (like public sector financial institutions).

5. **Auction to private entity** refers to transactions involving sales made by the Government in CPSEs through an auction to private entities.

6. **Sale to employees** refers to transactions involving sales made by the Government to employees of the respective CPSEs.

7. **Institutional placement programme** refers to transactions involving sales made by the Government through institutional placement programme in CPSEs

8. **Buyback** refers to transactions involving buyback of shares by the company from the Government

9. **Block deals/market sales** refers to transactions involving sales made by the Government through block deal or open market

10. **Exchange traded fund** was launched in 2014 by the GoI and comprises stock of listed CPSEs and approved to disinvest up to 3% of GoI shareholding from an individual CPSE. ETF is a security that tracks an index fund but trades like a stock on an exchange. Disinvestment through the ETF route allows simultaneous sale of GoI stake in various CPSEs across diverse sectors through a single offering. The Government operates two ETFs. (i) CPSE-ETF consisting of 12 CPSE stocks, and (ii) Bharat-22 ETF consisting of 16 CPSe stocks, 3 PSU banks, and 3 private sector stocks (ITC, L&T, and Axis).

Table A.2 Methodologies used for disinvestment of CPSEs from 1991–92 to 2020–21 (in crores of rupees)

Year	Strategic sale[1]	Public offer[2]	CPSE to CPSE sale[3]	Auction to-FIs[4]	Auction-private entity[5]	Sale to employee[6]	Institutional placement[7]	Buy back[8]	Block deals[9]	Exchange traded fund[10]	Total
1991–92				3037							3037
1992–93				1912							1912
1993–94											0.00
1994–95				4843							4843
1995–96				168							168
1996–97		379									379
1997–98		910									910
Total (FY 1992 to 98)		**1289**		**9962**							**11252**
1998–99		783	4182	404							5371
1999–00	105	1020	459								1584
2000–01	554		1317								1871
2001–02	2089		1153			25					3268
2002–03	2335					12					2347
2003–04	342	15128			77						15547
Total (FY 1999 to 04)	**5,427**	**16,932**	**7,113**	**404**	**77**	**37**					**29,990**
2004–05		2700				64					2764
2005–06				1567		2					1569
2006–07											0.00
2007–08		1814		2366							4181
2008–09											0.00
2009–10		21305	2247								23552
2010–11		22762									22762

Year										
2011–12		14035								14035
2012–13		23857								23857
2013–14		3102	5340		67	358	2131	7388	3000	21321
Total (FY 2005 to 14)		**89,578**	**7,587**	**3,934**	**77**	**358**	**2,131**	**7388**	**3,000**	**114,045**
2014–15		24277			71		4483	8790		24348
2015–16		19574			529		19026	4153	8500	24057
2016–17		7532	36915		315		5340	779	14500	44378
2017–18		38017	15913		17		10682	1881	45080	99241
2018–19		12590	13883		1		822	1,627	30869	85063
2019–20		1771			1		3,940			49228
2020–21	3,390									30213
Total (FY 2015 to 21)	**3,390**	**22,286**	**66,711**	**14,301**	**935**		**44,295**	**20,146**	**98,949**	**360,477**
GRAND TOTAL (FY 1992 to FY 2021)	**8,815**	**126,050**	**233,850**	**81,411**	**1,039**	**358**	**46,426**	**23,588**	**101,949**	**5,11,818**

Source: Created by author based on BSE PSU Data, Yearwise Summary of Past Disinvestments, accessed June 18, 2021, www.bsepsu.com/disinvest_database.asp#prettyPhoto[iframe]/10/

Appendix D

Table A.3 Privatised Central Public Sector Enterprises (CPSEs)

S.No.	Enterprise	Year privatised	Acquired by	Residual equity of GoI (in %)
1	Bharat Aluminium Company Ltd (BALCO)	2000–01	Sterlite Industries, a unit of Vedanta Resources	49
2	CMC Ltd (CMC)	2001–02	TCS	32.31
3	Hindustan Zinc Ltd (HZL)	2002–03, 2003–04	Sterlite Industries, a unit of Vedanta Resources	29.55
4	Hindustan Teleprinters Ltd (HTL)	2001–02	Himachal Futuristic Communications (HFCL)	26
5	Indian Petrochemicals Corporation Ltd (IPCL)	2002–03	Reliance Petro Investments	33.95
6	Jessop & Co. Ltd (Subsidiary of BBUNL)	2003–04	Indo-Wagon Engineering Ltd	27
7	Lagan Jute Machinery Co. Ltd (LJMC)	2000–01	Muralidhar Ratanlal Exports Ltd	26
8	Maruti Udyog Ltd (MUL)	2003–04, 2005–06, 2007–08	Suzuki	0
9	Modern Food Industries Ltd (MFIL)	1999–2000, & 2002–03	Hindustan Levers	0
10	Paradeep Phosphates Ltd (PPL)	2001–02	Zuari Maroc Phosphates Pvt Ltd	26
11	Videsh Sanchar Nigam Ltd (VSNL)	2001–02	Panatone Finvest (A Tata Group Co)	26

B. **Sale of hotels**

Hotel Ashok, Bangalore (ITDC) given on 30 year
lease-cum-management control
18 Hotel Units of ITDC –Privatised
(Details below)

	ITDC hotel details	Year	BUYER (Amount realised in crore of ₹)	Residual equity GoI
1	Hotel Agra – Ashok	2001–02	Mohan Singh (3.61)	0
2	Hotel Madurai –Ashok	2001–02	Sangu Chakra Hotels Pvt Ltd (4.98)	0
3	Hotel Bodhgaya – Ashok	2001–02	Lotus Nikku Hotels (1.81)	0
4	Hotel Hassan – Ashok	2001–02	Malnad Hotels & Resorts Pvt Ltd (2.27)	0
5	Temple Bay Ashok Beach, Mamallapuram	2001–02	G.R. Thangamaligai Pvt Ltd (6.13)	0
6	Qutab Hotel, New Delhi	2001–02	Consortium of Sushil Gupta & Others (34.45)	0
7	Lodhi Hotel, New Delhi	2001–02	Silverlink Holdings Ltd (71.93)	0
8	Laxmi Vilas Palace Hotel, Udaipur	2001–02	Bharat Hotels Ltd (6.77)	0
9	Hotel Manali Ashok	2002–03	Auto Impex Ltd (3.66)	0
10	Kovlam Ashok Beach Resort, Kovalam	2002–03	MFAR Hotels Ltd (40.38)	0
11	Hotel Aurangabad Ashok	2002–03	Loksangam Hotels & Resorts Pvt Ltd (16.50)	0

(continued)

Table A.3 Cont.

S.No.	Enterprise	Year privatised	Acquired by	Residual equity of GoI (in %)
12	Hotel Airport Ashok, Kolkata	2002–03	Bright Enterprises Pvt Ltd Consortium (19.39)	0
13	Hotel Khajuraho Ashok	2002–03	Bharat Hotels Ltd (2.19)	0
14	Hotel Varanasi Ashok	2002–03	Consortium of Ramnath Hotels (8.38)	0
15	Hotel Kanishka, New Delhi	2002–03	Nehru Place Hotels Ltd (92.38)	0
16	Hotel Indraprastha New Delhi	2002–03	Moral Trading & Investment Ltd (43.38)	0
17	Hotel Ranjit, New Delhi	2002–03	Consortium of Unison Hotels & Formax Commercial Pvt Ltd (29.28)	0
18	Punjab Hotel (ITDC & Chandigarh Adm.)	2002–03	Taj Gvk Hotels & Resorts Ltd (17.27)	0
Few hotels of Hotel Corporation of India, a subsidiary of Air India (disinvestment proceeds to Air India)				
1	Indo. Hokke Hotels Ltd, Rajgir	2001–02	Inpac Travels (India) Pvt Ltd (6.51)	0
2	Centaur Hotel Mumbai Airport	2002–03	Batra Hospitality Pvt Ltd (83.00)	0
3	Hotel Juhu, Mumbai	2001–02	Tulip Hospitality Pvt Ltd (153.00)	0

CPSE to CPSE sale

1	BONGAIGAON REFINERY & PETROCEMICALS LTD	2000–01	INDIAN OIL CORPORATION (148.80)	0
	IBP Ltd	2001–02, 2002–03, 2003–04	INDIAN OIL CORPORATION	0
2	DREDGING CORP. OF INDIA LTD	2018–19	VISHAKAPATNAM PORT TRUST, PARADEEP PORT TRUST, JAWAHARLAL NEHRU PORT TRUST & DEENDAYAL PORT TRUST (1049.17)	0
3	HINDUSTAN PETROLEUM CORP. LTD	2017–18	OIL & NATURAL GAS CORP.LTD (36,915.00)	0
4	HSCC (INDIA) LTD	2018–19	NBCC (INDIA) LTD (285.00)	0
5	KAMARAJAR PORT LTD	2019–20	CHENNAI PORT TRUST (2383.00)	0
6	KOCHI REFINERIES LTD	2000–01	BHARAT PETROLEUM CORP. LTD (659.10)	0
7	MADRAS REFINERIES LTD	2000–01	INDIAN OIL CORP. LTD (509.33)	0
8	NORTH EASTERN ELECTRIC POWER CORP.LTD(NEEPCO)	2019–20	NTPC LTD (4,000)	0
9	THDC INDIA LTD	2019–20	NTPC LTD (7,500)	0

Source: Created by author based on data given on website of DIPAMwww.dipam.gov.in/dipam/, and BSE PSU www.bsepsu.com/disinvest_database. asp

Appendix E

CPSEs 'in-principle' approved by Cabinet Committee on Economic Affairs for strategic disinvestment (date of approval in bracket)

ONGOING

1. Nagarnar Steel Plant of NMDC 27.10.2016
2. Alloy Steel Plant, Durgapur; Salem Steel Plant, and Bhadrwati units of SAIL, 27.10.2016
3. Ferro Scrap Nigam Ltd (Subsidiary) 27.10.2016
4. Central Electronics Ltd. 27.10.2016
5. Bharat Earth Movers Ltd (BEML) 27.10.2016
6. Cement Corporation of India Ltd. 27.10.2016
7. Bridge & Roof Co. India Ltd. 27.10.2016
8. Engineering Projects (India) Ltd. 27.10.2016
9. Scooters India Ltd 27.10.2016
10. Bharat Pumps & Compressors Ltd. 27.10.2016
11. Hindustan Newsprint Ltd (Subsidiary) 27.10.2016
12. Hindustan Fluorocarbons Ltd (Subsidiary) 27.10.2016
13. Pawan Hans Ltd. 27.10.2016
14. Projects Development India Ltd. 27.10.2016
15. Hindustan Prefab Ltd (HPL) 27.10.2016
16. Hindustan Antibiotics Ltd. 28.12.2016
17. Bengal Chemicals and Pharmaceuticals Limited (BCPL) 28.12.2016
18. Air India and its subsidiaries 28.06.2017
19. India Medicines & Pharmaceuticals Corporation Ltd (IMPCL) 01.11.2017
20. Karnataka Antibiotics and Pharmaceuticals Ltd. 01.11.2017
21. HLL Lifecare 01.11.2017
22. Kamarajar Port Limited 28.02.2019
23. Shipping Corporation of India (SCI) 20.11.2019

24. (a) Bharat Petroleum Corporation Ltd (except Numaligarh Refinery Limited) (b) BPCL stake in Numaligarh Refinery Limited to a CPSE strategic buyer 20.11.2019
25. Container Corporation of India Ltd (CONCOR) 20.11.2019
26. THDC India Limited (THDCIL) 20.11.2019
27. North Eastern Electric Power Corp. Ltd (NEEPCO) 20.11.2019
28. Neelanchal Ispat Nigam Ltd (NINL) 08.01.2020.

[NINL is a joint venture company in which four central public sector enterprises – MMTC, NMDC, BHEL, and MECON – besides two state PSUs of the Odisha state government – IPICOL and OMC – are shareholders]

Transactions completed

29. Hindustan Petroleum Corporation Limited 19.07.2017 (ONGC, another CPSE acquired 51.11% stake of HPCL in January 2018)
30. Rural Electrification Corporation Limited 06.12.2018 (Power Finance Corporation, another CPSE to acquire 52.63% stake of Rural Electrification)
31. Hospital Services Consultancy Corporation Limited (HSCC) 27.10.2016 (National Buildings Construction Corporation Limited (NBCC), another CPSE acquired 100% of HSCC in November 2018).
32. National Projects Construction Corporation Limited (NPCC) 27.10.2016 (WAPCOS, another PSE acquired 98.89% shares in NPCC Ltd in April 2019).
33. Dredging Corporation of India Limited 01.11.2017 (to a consortium of four government ports namely (Visakhapatnam Port Trust (VPT), Paradip Port Trust (PPT), Jawaharlal Nehru Port Trust (JNPT) and Deendayal Port Trust (DPT)

Source: Economic Survey 2019–20, Volume I, Chapter 9,' Privatization and Wealth Creation', p. 229, www.indiabudget.gov.in/budget2020-21/economicsurvey/doc/vol1chapter/echap09_vol1.pdf

Index